About This Book

Why is this topic important?

Organizational consulting generally has a broader focus than training. Whereas a trainer might develop people's understanding of team roles, a consultant might help a dysfunctional team function. Similarly, a trainer might deliver a workshop on developing good time management and productivity skills, whereas a consultant might be contracted to analyze and recognize workflow through a team or through an entire division or operating unit. There are clearly similarities between training and consulting—and the terms are often used interchangeably—but each has a unique focus and requires divergent approaches, tools, and techniques.

What can you achieve with this book?

Offering entirely new content each year, the consulting edition of *The Pfeiffer Annual* showcases the latest thinking and cutting-edge approaches to organization development and performance improvement contributed by practicing consultants, organizational systems experts, and academics. Designed for both the dedicated consultant and the training professional who straddles both roles, the *Annual* presents a unique source of new knowledge and ideas, as well as practical and proven applications for facilitating better work processes, implementing and sustaining change, and improving organizational effectiveness.

How is this book organized?

The book is divided into four sections: Experiential Learning Activities (ELAs); Editor's Choice; Inventories, Questionnaires, and Surveys; and Articles and Discussion Resources. The materials can be freely reproduced for use in the normal course of an assignment. ELAs are the mainstay of the *Annual* and cover a broad range of consulting topics. The activities are presented as complete and ready-to-use designs for working with groups; facilitator instructions and all necessary handouts and participant materials are included. Editor's Choice pieces allow us to select material that doesn't fit the other categories and take advantage of "hot topics." The instrument section introduces proven survey and assessment tools for gathering and sharing data on some aspect of performance. The articles section presents the best current thinking about workplace performance and organization development. Use these for your own professional development or as resources for working with others.

About Pfeiffer

Pfeiffer serves the professional development and hands-on resource needs of training and human resource practitioners and gives them products to do their jobs better. We deliver proven ideas and solutions from experts in HR development and HR management, and we offer effective and customizable tools to improve workplace performance. From novice to seasoned professional, Pfeiffer is the source you can trust to make yourself and your organization more successful.

Essential Knowledge Pfeiffer produces insightful, practical, and comprehensive materials on topics that matter the most to training and HR professionals. Our Essential Knowledge resources translate the expertise of seasoned professionals into practical, how-to guidance on critical workplace issues and problems. These resources are supported by case studies, worksheets, and job aids and are frequently supplemented with CD-ROMs, websites, and other means of making the content easier to read, understand, and use.

Essential Tools Pfeiffer's Essential Tools resources save time and expense by offering proven, ready-to-use materials—including exercises, activities, games, instruments, and assessments—for use during a training or team-learning event. These resources are frequently offered in looseleaf or CD-ROM format to facilitate copying and customization of the material.

Pfeiffer also recognizes the remarkable power of new technologies in expanding the reach and effectiveness of training. While e-hype has often created whizbang solutions in search of a problem, we are dedicated to bringing convenience and enhancements to proven training solutions. All our e-tools comply with rigorous functionality standards. The most appropriate technology wrapped around essential content yields the perfect solution for today's on-the-go trainers and human resource professionals.

Pfeiffer
www.pfeiffer.com

Essential resources for training and HR professionals

The Pfeiffer Annual Series

The *Pfeiffer Annuals* present each year never-before-published materials contributed by learning professionals and academics and written for trainers, consultants, and human resource and performance-improvement practitioners. As a forum for the sharing of ideas, theories, models, instruments, experiential learning activities, and best and innovative practices, the *Annuals* are unique, not least because only in the *Pfeiffer Annuals* will you find solutions from professionals like you who work in the field as trainers, consultants, facilitators, educators, and human resource and performance-improvement practitioners and whose contributions have been tried and perfected in real-life settings with actual participants and clients to meet real-world needs.

The Pfeiffer Annual: Consulting
Edited by Elaine Biech

The Pfeiffer Annual: Human Resource Management
Edited by Robert C. Preziosi

The Pfeiffer Annual: Training
Edited by Elaine Biech

Call for Papers

How would you like to be published in the *Pfeiffer Training* or *Consulting Annual*? Possible topics for submissions include group and team building, organization development, leadership, problem solving, presentation and communication skills, consulting and facilitation, and training-the-trainer. Contributions may be in one of the following three formats:

- Experiential Learning Activities

- Inventories, Questionnaires, and Surveys

- Articles and Discussion Resources

To receive a copy of the submission packet, which explains the requirements and will help you determine format, language, and style to use, contact editor Elaine Biech at Pfeifferannual@ aol.com or by calling 757-588-3939.

Elaine Biech, EDITOR

The *2006*
Pfeiffer
ANNUAL

CONSULTING

Pfeiffer
A Wiley Imprint
www.pfeiffer.com

ISBN-10: 0-7879-7820-5
ISBN-13: 978-0-7879-7822-8
ISSN: 1046-333-X

Acquiring Editor: Martin Delahoussaye
Director of Development: Kathleen Dolan Davies
Developmental Editor: Susan Rachmeler
Production Editor: Dawn Kilgore
Editor: Rebecca Taff
Manufacturing Supervisor: Becky Carreño
Editorial Assistant: Leota Higgins
Composition and Technical Art: Leigh McLellan Design

Printed in the United States of America

Printing   10 9 8 7 6 5 4 3 2 1

Contents

Experiential Learning Activities

Editor's Choice

Inventories, Questionnaires, and Surveys

Articles and Discussion Resources

**Topic is cutting edge

Preface

Beyond Your Own Little World

Worldly wisdom. Those two words continued to buzz in my brain as we read, selected, and edited the submissions during the past nine months for the *2006 Training* and *Consulting Annuals.* Why? Was it that we had more international submissions than ever before? No. I didn't think that was it, even though four of the submissions from Canada, India, New Zealand, and Spain made the final cut.

After some thought, I decided that it was based on the unique variety of submissions. I think you will agree. The *2006 Annuals* offer contributions from music, art, and literature ("Pygmalion" and "El Quixote"). Many of the most interesting submissions in the two volumes test the boundaries of your comfort zones, encouraging you to address difficult subjects such as trust, values, narcissism, and your personal life plan.

Today's trainers, consultants, and facilitators require a broader variety of skills, expertise, and knowledge. To gain new skills, to acquire different expertise, and to attain worldly wisdom requires that you push yourself outside your comfort zone beyond your own little world. This is hard work! But it is just what we all need to become better at what we do for our customers, our employers, and our clients. We need to learn and grow—and to achieve a more global mindset.

Experiential learning activities in these two volumes test how far you are willing to stretch (try Jameson's relay race). Articles in these two volumes provide you with new ways to consider old topics (read Royal's article addressing buy-in). Instruments in the two volumes help you measure your individual development as well as leadership and organizational effectiveness.

What about beyond the *Annuals?* What personal attributes does it take to continue to learn and grow to keep you on top of the changes and the expectations of your profession? Peter Drucker tells us that we cannot manage change, we can only stay ahead of it. Change creates an environment that forces us to move from our comfortable world to a more comprehensive (or global) mindset. It means that we must continue to learn and grow to stay ahead of change.

The following personal attributes identify perspectives that I have learned from other professionals, my colleagues, and you, our *Annual* contributors. Think about yourself as you read them. What can you do to boost your worldly wisdom?

Know yourself. Know your strengths. Know your weaknesses. Know your limitations. Turn your weaknesses into strengths through learning and experience. Invite others to provide their insight and feedback.

Welcome crises. You will learn more from the surprises that life brings your way than from any book. Be flexible and innovate. Creative solutions are the mark of a wise and flexible person.

Take risks. The more you risk, the greater your chances for success or failure. Risks abound in everything you do, but the riskiest of all is to never take a risk. Risks, and yes, sometimes failure, are a strong foundation for learning.

Stretch. Try the impossible. Eleanor Roosevelt said, "You must do the thing you think you cannot do." Anything is possible. You will never know if you do not try. *Feel the Fear and Do It Anyway,* is one of my favorite book titles. It states what we all must consider before we say "can't."

Broaden your perspective. If you are a big picture thinker, learn to take care of the details. If you are creative, practice logic. If you focus on tasks, take time to focus on people. Focus on both the future and on the history that created it. Argue for and against the same issue. Each of you has natural preferences. Spend time in the opposite mode to help you step outside your comfortable world.

Exude passion. Life is simply too short to do something you do not like. I hope that you not only *like* what you do—I hope you *love* what you do. I do not believe that anyone should get up and go to work in the morning; I believe that we should all get up and go to play every morning. If you are not playing every day, learn something new, try a new process, meet a new colleague or client. Find something that paints the passion back in the picture.

Know when to quit. Training, consulting, facilitating are all rewarding professions. But when they no longer are rewarding to you, quit. When play becomes work; when fun becomes drudgery; when challenges become formidable obstacles, recognize that it may be time for you to move on.

This is certainly not an exhaustive list of every attribute that will move you to experience the wide world around you, but it is a place to start. And be sure to use the *2006 Annuals* to help you start.

A Native American friend shared a quote he attributed to his people. It has echoed in my mind for years, "If you are not living on the edge, you take up too much room." To gain worldly wisdom, we all probably need to do more edge-sitting outside the box in which we find comfort.

What Are the *Annuals*?

The *Annual* series is published in two volumes: Training and Consulting. The collection of practical materials is written for trainers, consultants, and performance-improvement technologists. We know the materials are practical, because they are written by the same practitioners who use the materials.

The *Pfeiffer Annual: Training* focuses on skill building and knowledge enhancement and also includes cutting-edge articles that enhance the skills and professional development of trainers. The *Pfeiffer Annual: Consulting* focuses on intervention techniques and organizational systems. It also includes skill building for the professional consultant. You can read more about the differences between the two volumes in the section that follows this preface, "The Difference Between Training and Consulting: Which Annual to Use."

The *Annuals* have been an inspirational source for experiential learning activities, resource for instruments, and reference for cutting-edge material for thirty-four years. Whether you are a trainer, a consultant, a facilitator, or a bit of each, you will find tools and resources that provide you with the basics and challenge (and we hope inspire) you to use new techniques and models.

Annual Loyalty

The *Pfeiffer Annual* series has many loyal subscribers. There are several reasons for this loyalty. In addition to the wide variety of topics and implementation levels, the *Annuals* provide materials that are applicable to varying circumstances. You will find instruments for individuals, teams, and organizations; experiential learning activities to round out workshops, team building, or consulting assignments; ideas and contemporary solutions for managing human capital; and articles that increase your own knowledge base, to use as reference materials in your writing, or as a source of ideas for your training or consulting assignments.

Many of our readers have been loyal customers for a dozen or more years. If you are one of them, we thank you. And we encourage each of you to give back to the profession by submitting a sample of your work to share with your colleagues.

The *Annuals* owe most of their success, though, to the fact that they are immediately ready to use. All of the materials may be duplicated for educational and training purposes. If you need to adapt or modify the materials to tailor them for your audience's needs, go right ahead. We only request that the credit statement found on the copyright page (and on each reproducible page) be retained on all copies. Our liberal copyright policy makes it easy and fast for you to use the materials to do your job.

However, if you intend to reproduce the materials in publications for sale or if you wish to reproduce more than one hundred copies of any one item, please contact us for prior written permission.

If you are a new *Annual* user, welcome! If you like what you see in the 2006 edition, you may want to consider subscribing to a standing order. By doing so, you are guaranteed to receive your copy each year straight off the press and receive a discount off the cover price. And if you want to go back and have the entire series for your use, then the *Pfeiffer Library*—which contains content from the very first edition to the present day—is available on CD-ROM. You can find information on the *Pfeiffer Library* at www.pfeiffer.com.

I often refer to many of my *Annuals* from the 1980s. They include several classic activities that have become a mainstay in my team-building designs. But most of all, the *Annuals* have been a valuable resource for over thirty years because the materials come from professionals like you who work in the field as trainers, consultants, facilitators, educators, and performance-improvement technologists, whose contributions have been tried and perfected in real-life settings with actual participants and clients to meet real-world needs.

To this end, we encourage you to submit materials to be considered for publication. We are interested in receiving experiential learning activities; inventories, questionnaires, and surveys; and articles and discussion resources. Contact the Pfeiffer Editorial Department at the address listed on the copyright page for copies of our guidelines for contributors or contact me directly at Box 8249, Norfolk, VA 23503, or by email at pfeifferannual @aol.com. We welcome your comments, ideas, and contributions.

Acknowledgments

Thank you to the dedicated, friendly, thoughtful people at Pfeiffer who produced the *2006 Pfeiffer Annual: Consulting*: Kathleen Dolan Davies, Martin Delahoussaye, Leota Higgins, Dawn Kilgore, Susan Rachmeler, Laura Reizman, and Rebecca Taff. Thank you to Lorraine Kohart of ebb associates inc, who assisted our authors with the many submission details and who ensured that we met all the deadlines.

Most important, thank you to our contributors, who have once again shared their ideas, techniques, and materials so that trainers and consultants everywhere may benefit. Won't you consider joining the ranks of these prestigious professionals?

Elaine Biech
Editor
September 2005

The Difference Between Training and Consulting
Which Annual to Use?

The two volumes of the *Pfeiffer Annuals*—training and consulting—are resources for two different but closely related professions. Each *Annual* serves as a collection of tools and support materials used by the professionals in their respective arenas. The volumes include activities, articles, and instruments used by individuals in the training and consulting fields. The training volume is written with the trainer in mind, and the consulting volume is written with the consultant in mind.

How can you differentiate between the two volumes? Let's begin by defining each profession.

A *trainer* can be defined as anyone who is responsible for designing and delivering knowledge to adult learners and may include an internal HRD professional employed by an organization or an external practitioner who contracts with an organization to design and conduct training programs. Generally, the trainer is a subject-matter expert who is expected to transfer knowledge so that the trainee can know or do something new. A *consultant* is someone who provides unique assistance or advice (based on what the consultant knows or has experienced) to someone else, usually known as "the client." The consultant may not necessarily be a subject-matter expert in all situations. Often the consultant is an expert at using specific tools to extract, coordinate, resolve, organize, expedite, or implement an organizational situation.

The lines between the consulting and training professions have blurred in the past few years. First, the names and titles have blurred. For example, some external trainers call themselves "training consultants" as a way of distinguishing themselves from internal trainers. Some organizations now have internal consultants, who usually reside in the training department. Second, the roles have blurred. While a consultant has always been expected to deliver measurable results, now trainers are expected to do so as well. Both are expected to improve performance; both are expected to contribute to the bottom line. Facilitation was at one time thought to be a consultant skill; today trainers are expected to use facilitation skills to train. Training one-on-one was a trainer skill; today consultants train executives one-on-one and call it "coaching." The introduction of the "performance technologist," whose role is one of combined trainer and consultant, is a perfect example of a new profession that has evolved due to the need for trainers to use more "consulting" techniques in their work. The "performance consultant" is a new role supported by the American Society for Training and Development (ASTD). ASTD has shifted its focus from training to performance improvement.

As you can see, the roles and goals of training and consulting are not nearly as specific as they once may have been. However, when you step back and examine the two professions from a big-picture perspective, you can more easily differentiate between the two. Maintaining a big-picture focus will also help you determine which *Pfeiffer Annual* to turn to as your first resource.

Both volumes cover the same general topics: communication, teamwork, problem solving, and leadership. However, depending on your requirement and purpose—a training or consulting need—you will use each in different situations. You will select the *Annual* based on *how you will interact with the topic, not on what the topic might be.* Let's take a topic such as teamwork, for example. If you are searching for a lecturette that teaches the advantages of teamwork, a workshop activity that demonstrates the skill of making decisions in a team, or a handout that discusses team stages, look to the Training *Annual.* On the other hand, if you are conducting a team-building session for a dysfunctional team, helping to form a new team, or trying to understand the dynamics of an executive team, you will look to the Consulting *Annual.*

The Training Annual

The materials in the Training volume focus on skill building and knowledge enhancement as well as on the professional development of trainers. They generally focus on controlled events: a training program, a conference presentation, a classroom setting. Look to the Training *Annual* to find ways to improve a training session for 10 to 1,000 people and anything else that falls in the human resource development category:

- Specific experiential learning activities that can be built into a training program;
- Techniques to improve training: debriefing exercises, conducting role plays, managing time;
- Topical lecturettes;
- Ideas to improve a boring training program;

- Icebreakers and energizers for a training session;

- Surveys that can be used in a classroom;

- Ideas for moving an organization from training to performance; and

- Ways to improve your skills as a trainer.

The Consulting Annual

The materials in the Consulting volume focus on intervention techniques and organizational systems as well as on the professional development of consultants. They generally focus on "tools" that you can have available just in case: concepts about organizations and their development (or demise) and about more global situations. Look to the Consulting *Annual* to find ways to improve consulting activities from team building and executive coaching to organization development and strategic planning:

- Skills for working with executives;

- Techniques for solving problems, effecting change, and gathering data;

- Team-building tools, techniques, and tactics;

- Facilitation ideas and methods;

- Processes to examine for improving an organization's effectiveness;

- Surveys that can be used organizationally; and

- Ways to improve your effectiveness as a consultant.

Summary

Even though the professions and the work are closely related and at times interchangeable, there is a difference. Use the following table to help you determine which *Annual* you should scan first for help. Remember, however, there is some blending of the two and either *Annual* may have your answer. It depends . . .

Element	Training	Consulting
Topics	Teams, Communication, Problem Solving	Teams, Communication, Problem Solving
Topic Focus	Individual, Department	Corporate, Global
Purpose	Skill Building, Knowledge Transfer	Coaching, Strategic Planning, Building Teams
Recipient	Individuals, Departments	Usually More Organizational
Organizational Level	All Workforce Members	Usually Closer to the Top
Delivery Profile	Workshops, Presentations	Intervention, Implementation
Atmosphere	Structured	Unstructured
Time Frame	Defined	Undefined
Organizational Cost	Moderate	High
Change Effort	Low to Moderate	Moderate to High
Setting	Usually a Classroom	Anywhere
Professional Experience	Entry Level, Novice	Proficient, Master Level
Risk Level	Low	High
Professional Needs	Activities, Resources	Tools, Theory
Application	Individual Skills	Usually Organizational System

When you get right down to it, we are all trainers and consultants. The skills may cross over. A great trainer is also a skilled consultant. And a great consultant is also a skilled trainer. The topics may be the same, but how you implement them may be vastly different. Which *Annual* to use? Remember to think about your purpose in terms of the big picture: consulting or training.

As you can see, we have both covered.

Introduction
to *The 2006 Pfeiffer Annual: Consulting*

Getting the Most from This Resource

The *2006 Pfeiffer Annual: Consulting* is the latest addition to a series that has been in print since 1972. The *Annual* offers a collection of practical and useful materials for professionals in the broad area of human resource development (HRD).

The materials are written by and for professionals, including trainers, organization-development and organization-effectiveness consultants, performance-improvement technologists, facilitators, educators, instructional designers, and others.

Each *Annual* has three main sections: experiential learning activities; inventories, questionnaires, and surveys; and articles and discussion resources. A fourth section, editor's choice, has been reserved for those unique contributions that do not fit neatly into one of the three main sections, but are valuable as identified by the editorial staff. Each published submission is classified in one of the following categories: Individual Development, Communication, Problem Solving, Groups, Teams, Consulting, Facilitating, Leadership, and Organizations. Within each category, pieces are further classified into logical subcategories, which are identified in the introductions to the three sections.

"Cutting edge" topics are identified in each *Annual.* This designation highlights topics that present information, concepts, tools, or perspectives that may be recent additions to the profession or that have not previously appeared in the *Annual* or are currently "hot topics."

The series continues to provide an opportunity for HRD professionals who wish to share their experiences, their viewpoints, and their processes with their colleagues.

To that end, Pfeiffer publishes guidelines for potential authors. These guidelines are available from the Pfeiffer Editorial Department in San Francisco, California.

Materials are selected for the *Annuals* based on the quality of the ideas, applicability to real-world concerns, relevance to current HRD issues, clarity of presentation, and ability to enhance our readers' professional development. In addition, we choose experiential learning activities that will create a high degree of enthusiasm among the participants and add enjoyment to the learning process. As in the past several years, the contents of each *Annual* span a wide range of subject matter, reflecting the range of interests of our readers.

Our contributor list includes a wide selection of experts in the field: in-house practitioners, consultants, and academically based professionals. A list of contributors to the *Annual* can be found at the end of the volume, including their names, affiliations, addresses, telephone numbers, facsimile numbers, and email addresses. Readers will find this list useful if they wish to locate the authors of specific pieces for feedback, comments, or questions. Further information on each contributor is presented in a brief biographical sketch that appears at the conclusion of each article. We publish this information to encourage "networking," which continues to be a valuable mainstay in the field of human resource development.

We are pleased with the high quality of material that is submitted for publication each year and often regret that we have page limitations. In addition, just as we cannot publish every manuscript we receive, you may find that not all published works are equally useful to you. Therefore, we encourage and invite ideas, materials, and suggestions that will help us to make subsequent *Annuals* as useful as possible to all of our readers.

Introduction
to the Experiential Learning Activities Section

Experiential learning activities ensure that lasting learning occurs. They should be selected with a specific learning objective in mind. These objectives are based on the participants' needs and the facilitator's skills. Although the experiential learning activities presented here all vary in goals, group size, time required, and process, they all incorporate one important element: questions that ensure learning has occurred. This discussion, led by the facilitator, assists participants to process the activity, to internalize the learning, and to relate it to their day-to-day situations. It is this element that creates the unique learning experience and learning opportunity that only an experiential learning activity can bring to the group process.

Readers have used the *Annuals'* experiential learning activities for years to enhance their training and consulting events. Each learning experience is complete and includes all lecturettes, handout content, and other written material necessary to facilitate the activity. In addition, many include variations of the design that the facilitator might find useful. If the activity does not fit perfectly with your objective, within your time frame, or to your group size, we encourage you to adapt the activity by adding your own variations. You will find additional experiential learning activities listed in the "Experiential Learning Activities Categories" chart that immediately follows this introduction.

The 2006 Pfeiffer Annual: Consulting includes twelve activities, in the following categories:

Individual Development: Sensory Awareness

Presuppositions: Enhancing Performance and Perspective, by Devora D. Zack

Individual Development: Diversity

Honored Strangers: Exploring What New Immigrants Experience, by Edwina Pio

Individual Development: Life/Career Planning

Windows: Demonstrating Group Competencies, by Beverly J. Bitterman

Communication: Building Trust

Trust ARCH: Building Team Support, by Mary B. Wacker

Communication: Conflict

The Team Circle: Moving from Conflict to Harmony, by Bridget A. O'Brien

Communication: Styles

Beyond I, Me, and My: Honoring Separate Realities,
by Marilyn J. Sprague-Smith

Problem Solving: Generating Alternatives

Pass the Solution, Please: Brainstorming Suggestions, by Gail Hahn

Groups: How Groups Work

Empowerment: Ensuring the Basics Are in Place, by Chris W. Chen

Teams: How Groups Work

Your Fantasy Work Team: Building a Perfect Team, by Peter R. Garber

Teams: Roles

Lights, Camera, Action! Creating Team Commercials, by Cher Holton

Consulting, Training, and Facilitating: Facilitating: Closing

The Web We Weave: Closing the Team's Work, by Kristin J. Arnold

Organizations: Vision, Mission, Values, and Strategy

Towers: Preventing Business Failure, by Cheryl A. Brown

To further assist you in selecting appropriate ELAs, we provide the following grid that summarizes category, time required, group size, and risk factor for each ELA.

Category	ELA Title	Page	Time Required	Group Size	Risk Factor
Individual Development: Sensory Awareness	Presuppostitions: Enhancing Performance and Perspective	11	65 minutes	Teams of 3 to 6	Moderate
Individual Development: Diversity	Honored Strangers: Exploring What New Immigrants Experience	19	Approximately 90 minutes	12 to 15	Moderate to High
Individual Development: Life/Career Planning	Windows: Demonstrating Group Competencies	29	4 to 6 hours over 1 to 2 weeks	Management group, plus teams of 4 to 10	Moderate
Communication: Building Trust	Trust ARCH: Building Team Support	37	Approximately 90 minutes	Groups of 4 to 6	ModeratE to High
Communication: Conflict	The Team Circle: Moving from Conflict to Harmony	45	30 to 45 minutes, plus pre-work	8 to 10 members of an intact team	Moderate
Communication: Styles	Beyond I, Me, and My: Honoring Separate Realities	55	45 minutes	Groups of 5 or 7	Low
Problem Solving: Generating Alternatives	Pass the Solution, Please: Brainstorming Suggestions	67	Approximately 60 minutes	Unlimited groups of 5 to 8	Moderate
Groups: How Groups Work	Empowerment: Ensuring the Basics Are in Place	71	60 minutes	Six or more groups of 5 to 7	Moderate
Teams: How Groups Work	Your Fantasy Work Team: Building a Perfect Team	83	40 to 50 minutes	Any size	Moderate
Teams: Roles	Lights, Camera, Action! Creating Team Commercials	89	60 to 90 minutes	Two or more groups of 4 to 10	Moderate
Consulting, Training, and Facilitating: Facilitating: Closing	The Web We Weave: Closing the Team's Work	93	10 to 20 minutes	5 or more	Moderate
Organizations: Vision, Mission, Values, Strategy	Towers: Preventing Business Failure	97	70 to 80 minutes	Groups of 3 to 5	Low

Experiential Learning Activities Categories

Note that numbering system was discontinued beginning with the 2004 *Annuals*.

Presuppositions
Enhancing Performance and Perspective

Activity Summary

An interactive, small-group activity providing participants with the tools to reframe their perceptions, leading to improved outlook and productivity.

Goals

- To learn about and understand NLP (neurolinguistic programming).

- To apply NLP to enhancing one's work life and relationships.

- To develop the ability to choose positive responses to events.

Group Size

Any size group in teams of 3 to 6 persons each.

Time Required

65 minutes.

Materials

- One Presuppositions Handout per participant.

- One Presuppositions Recommended Readings per participant.

- Blank paper and a pen for each participant.

- Flip chart with felt-tipped markers.

Physical Setting

A space large enough for teams to work seated in groups of 3 to 6, ideally around tables.

Facilitating Risk Rating

Moderate.

Process

1. Introduce the session by explaining that participants will be applying neuro-linguistic programming-based presuppositions to enhance their work lives and perceptions. Break the group into smaller teams of 3 to 6 at tables.

2. Distribute copies of the Presuppositions Handout, blank paper, and pens to participants. Ask each table group to spend time acquainting themselves with the Presuppositions in a way that each team selects (reading quietly, taking turns reading aloud, or selecting a single reader).
   (10 minutes.)

3. When the teams complete that task, field any questions that arise; then reinforce these key points:

   • Presuppositions are not necessarily true. Their value is not in debating "reality" but in deciding to live "as if" they are true and to note the impact they can have on one's work, effectiveness, and rapport with others.

   • While setting the goal of living as if presuppositions are true may seem simple, it is in fact a challenging endeavor that requires constant attention and commitment. The potential impact can be quite powerful.

   • Each participant will select one presupposition to focus on during the session and over the next two weeks. Encourage everyone to pick one that resonates with him or her and/or one that seems particularly pertinent to a current challenge. If someone wishes to create his or her own presupposition, encourage the person to do so.
   (10 minutes.)

4. Assign an additional 15 minutes of group time for participants to individually select presuppositions and then to share the following in teams:

   • Why the person picked that particular presupposition.

- How he or she interprets the presupposition.

- How he or she envisions a potential impact from living as if it were true.

Let the group know when half the time has elapsed and again when two minutes remain. Remind them at these intervals to ensure that everyone has a chance to share.

(15 minutes.)

5. After the teams share in their small groups, open up the discussion to the whole room, asking:

- Does anyone wish to share comments or ideas from the smaller teams that may be pertinent to everyone? (Note key points on the flip chart at the front of the room and post if desired.)

- Did team members interpret presuppositions differently? What were some of the differences, and what was the impact of having different interpretations?

- If anyone chose to make up a new presupposition, what was it?

- How can you apply your presupposition to challenging relationships? Crisis management? Dealing with matters outside your control? Task accomplishment? Other applications?

- How have you lived in the past that was counter to the presuppositions you chose? What was the impact? What could you do differently now?

- What assumptions have you made in the past about other people that could change through the lens of a presupposition?

(20 minutes.)

6. Ask participants to each choose an "accountability partner" with whom to check in within the next two weeks. Partners should select a time and means of speaking (in person, by phone, via email) at that time. Their follow-up conversations should include asking each other whether they were able to integrate the presuppositions into their processing of events and the impact it had if so. They may at that time, if they choose, decide with the partner to select second presuppositions and agree to speak again in the future.

7. Lead a concluding discussion that could include some or all of the following questions:

- How could adopting presuppositions into your thinking impact your work life?

- How much control do we have over how we process and respond to external events?

- Why is it important to revisit your presupposition with your accountability partner in two weeks?

- In what ways could you apply what you learned to any challenging work relationships?

  (10 minutes.)

8. Remind participants that we can impact our reality through choosing our responses.

9. Conclude by distributing the Presuppositions Recommended Readings for those inspired to learn more about NLP.

Submitted by Devora D. Zack.

Devora D. Zack, *president, OCC, specializes in leadership, teams, communication, and change. Her seminars, assessments, and coaching result in lasting change for dozens of clients. Her clients include Deloitte, IRS, AOL, Cornell, DHS, IMF, OPM, and AmeriCorps. She is certified in neurolinguistic programming and the Myers-Briggs Type Indicator. She holds an MBA from Cornell University and a BA from The University of Pennsylvania. Her company recently won USDA's Woman-Owned Business of the Year award.*

Presuppositions Handout

Presuppositions come from neurolinguistic programming, a field of applied psychology that teaches through language, action, and perceptions how to achieve excellence in communication, relationships, and influence.

Presuppositions are not necessarily true. However, they are useful beliefs for effective inter- and intra-personal communication. Choosing to interact *as if they are true* can have a powerful impact on your attitudes toward others and on your own effectiveness. The following presuppositions (assumptions) are made in NLP:

A. *The meaning of your communication is the response that you have, independent of intention.* By taking responsibility for the "communication loop," you increase your ability to change your behavior and your reactions to others' responses.

B. *There is no such thing as failure, only feedback and results.* "Failure" or "mistakes" are destructive labels. Instead, setbacks can be utilized to achieve a goal by perceiving them as information that was gained or as signals to learn more about a topic. "Failure" is really just information that gives us an opportunity to increase our effectiveness.

C. *People have the resources to accomplish their goals.* Clarify the underlying intention you have for achieving your goal. Our resources include the abilities, attitudes, and emotions that assist us in achieving what we want. If we lack a resource, we can combine it with others, redefine our need, or assess other ways to obtain the necessary skills.

D. *The map is not just the territory.* Our understanding and perception of the world create our own maps. These maps allow us to navigate through difficult experiences and rough "terrain"; however, our maps are not objective reflections of the world. As an analogy, a city map is a piece of paper with lines, words, and colors; it is not the city itself. The meaning we assign to our experience is the map; the experience is the territory.

E. *There's always another choice.* Every experience can be described in at least three different ways from three different perspectives (first, second, and third person). By changing perspective, you increase your information and alter your perceptions. This increases your possible choices. Even when it is difficult to see, hear, or feel them, there are other options.

Exercise

Select the presupposition above (A through E) (or create your own) that most resonates with you or has the most immediately relevant application to your life. Discuss in your group how your interpretation of the presupposition could lead to an enriching or alternative perspective on a current challenge you are experiencing, on your work life, and/or on your typical interactive style.

Presuppositions Recommended Readings

This list is for participants interested in learning more about neurolinguistic programming. Presuppositions are just one aspect of the diverse and fascinating field of NLP and its offshoot, NeuroSemantics. There are countless volumes on neurolinguistic programming. The items below have been selected because of their quality, accessibility, relevance to the workplace, and ease of application.

Bandler, R., & Grinder, J. (1980). *Reframing: Neurolinguistic programming and the transformation of meaning.* Salt Lake City, UT: Real People Press. (Note: This is the original text in the field of NLP.)

Charvet, S.R. (1997). *Words that change minds.* Dubuque, IA: Kendall/Hunt.

Knight, S. (1998). *NLP at work.* London, UK: Nicholas Brealey.

O'Connor, J., & Seymour, J. (1990). *Introducing neurolinguistic programming.* San Francisco, CA: HarperCollins.

Honored Strangers
Exploring What New Immigrants Experience

Activity Summary

An exploratory activity designed to assist participants/organizations to understand the immigrant experience and thereby enhance cross-cultural understanding and diversity management.

Goals

- To develop participants' awareness of the experience of immigrating to a new country.

- To increase cross-cultural understanding.

- To discover strategies to enhance diversity management.

Group Size

12 to 15 participants.

Time Required

Approximately 90 minutes.

Materials

- A set of 3" x 5" or 5" x 7" cards with "A," "B," or "C" written on them, so that each participant receives one card, in order to form three groups randomly (A's are the immigrants, B's are the host country individuals who were immigrants themselves, although they have been in the new country for some time, and C's will be the host country individuals with the ethnicity of the majority culture).

- Labels for the tables.

- A map of the world.

- One copy of the Honored Strangers Lecturette for the facilitator and copies to hand out to participants.

- One copy of the appropriate Honored Strangers Instruction Sheet for each participant.

- One copy of the Honored Strangers Bibliography for each participant.

- A flip chart and felt-tipped markers.

- Pens or pencils and blank paper for each participant.

Physical Setting

A large room so that each of the three groups is able to sit together, either at a table or in a circle.

Facilitating Risk Rating

Moderate to High.

Trainer's Note

The issue of immigration, ethnic minorities, and the majority culture in the workforce is a challenging one that individuals and organizations struggle with. It is important to introduce and address the issue of "honored strangers" and ways to integrate them into the workforce. The creation of a safe training milieu will give participants an opportunity to explore, understand, and develop strategies for incorporating new immigrants into the workplace.

It is possible to use this activity in an induction program, as part of an executive development program, or for organizations engaged in enhancing their diversity management strategies.

Process

1. In preparation for the workshop, set up three tables with an equal number of chairs around each table and a label (A, B, or C), so that the participants can be divided into three groups readily. Put the world map in a prominent place so that it can be seen by all the participants.

2. When participants arrive, randomly give each a card (having A, B, or C on it). Have them sit at the appropriate tables.

3. Ask participants to introduce themselves within their table groups, indicating on the world map their country of origin or ancestral homes.
   (15 minutes.)

4. Present the brief lecturette, which is on international population mobility and the multicultural workforce.
   (10 minutes.)

5. Hand each participant an Honored Strangers Instruction Sheet, giving the appropriate sheets to the "immigrant group" and the other sets of instructions to the host country groups. Have participants prepare their presentations. Provide a 10-minute warning.
   (30 minutes.)

6. Ask each group to present its 5-minute summary.
   (20 minutes.)

7. Lead a discussion to close this activity using the following questions:

   - What have you learned from this activity?

   - What could your organization do to improve the immigrant experience on the job?

   - What is your responsibility in this?

   - What will you do differently when you return to work?
   (15 minutes.)

8. Urge participants to take advantage of what they have experienced and learned so that immigrants become honored strangers. Bid participants farewell and give each a copy of the lecturette and a copy of the Honored Strangers Bibliography to take with them.
   (5 minutes.)

Variation

A reading assignment on diversity management or cross-cultural understanding can be completed prior to the workshop.

Submitted by Edwina Pio.

Edwina Pio, *Ph.D., has contributed to the* Annuals *for the past two years. A management educator and consultant, she has worked with groups in Asia, North America, Europe, and New Zealand. Her research is located at the intersections of management, psychology, and spirituality, with a focus on diversity issues in the workplace. Currently she lives in New Zealand, where she is an integral part of the business faculty of the Auckland University of Technology. She is also a registered counsellor and works with migrants.*

Honored Strangers Lecturette

Around 175 million persons currently reside outside the country of their birth, or approximately 3 percent of the world population. In fact, almost one out of every ten persons living in the more developed regions is an immigrant to that region. In the period 1995–2000, North American absorbed 1.4 million immigrants annually, followed by Europe with 0.8 million, and then by Oceania, with a net intake of 90,000 immigrants annually.

Immigration, often due to war, seeking work, and freedom to worship, has been a significant driver of population mobility across national borders. This mobility has increased over the last ten years and has resulted in a multicultural workforce in many parts of the world. While such a workforce has the potential for increased innovation and new mental models, it also can mean increasing tensions and conflict at work. While there are many laws, norms, standards, conventions, and recommendations with minimum standards that regulate conditions for workers in the industrial world, various perceptions of others in the workforce can make integrating immigrants into the workforce a minefield that one has to tread in delicately.

Research indicates that a number of psychological and social processes are involved when immigrants move to a new country, and how the immigrant stranger is honored in the culture sets the tone for future encounters, including how the immigrant is absorbed into the workforce. Every immigrant experiences some amount of culture shock in the new country based on his or her own mental software and background. In many cases, some of the simplest things have to be learned, for example, driving on the right-hand or left-hand side of the road, style of dress, ways of greeting one another, shopping habits, and work norms.

Acculturation is a longitudinal, dynamic social process that results in a change in a range of behaviors, attitudes, and values as the immigrant comes into contact with the host culture. Acculturation can be seen to consist of four stages: the first phase is the *honeymoon* or *euphoric stage,* followed by *culture shock* when real life starts in the new environment, especially on the job. This is one of the most challenging periods for both the immigrant and the organization. This is when the maximum help is needed to teach the immigrant and fellow workers the difference between them in terms of work norms and behavior. Obviously, the culture shock phase is environment specific and may be more or less apparent.

The third phase, sometimes referred to as the *acculturation phase,* is when the immigrant learns to function under the new conditions and has adopted some of the local behaviors with increasing self-confidence. The fourth phase is the *stable state* and depends in large part on how long the previous phases took and the intercultural encounters therein. In the stable phase, the immigrant can either be neutral, positive, or negative about the whole experience. Undoubtedly it is the mission of the organization to move the immigrant into a positive stable state as soon as possible.

It is important to realize that intercultural contact among workers does not automatically breed mutual understanding. In fact, it often confirms stereotypes! The creation of an environment in which people can meet and mix as equals requires a great deal more than just intercultural interaction. People may require training related to how to involve themselves with different cultural mores and how to demonstrate professional effectiveness, coupled with counseling to assist with personal and family adjustment to the new culture.

Many immigrants become marginal people who move between two worlds, as they alternate between the world of work in the new culture and their native culture in their own homes, sometimes leading them to operate on the periphery of society. In many cases it is easier for an immigrant if there is an already established ethnic community in the new country, which serves as a source of support and networking. It is also necessary for the host country to have some understanding of the special skills and experiences of the immigrants.

Organizations are faced with numerous challenges as they attempt to retain a multicultural workforce and remain competitive in the international economy. Much evidence points to the fact that successful acculturation depends heavily on how individual immigrants adjust to the culture and norms of the host country. The key factors in this adjustment are the training the immigrant receives, the demographic characteristics of the individual (family status, amount of previous international exposure, age), the disposition and personality of the individual, cultural flexibility, level of ethnocentricity—the belief that the values of one's own culture are superior to those held by people in other cultures—level of technical competence, and the level of perceived organizational support for becoming accepted into the new culture.

As organizations grapple with diversity management, there is a need to first identify immigrant issues, next to develop appropriate policies and practices for their acculturation, then to implement policies that support a diverse workforce, followed by the maintenance and monitoring of such policies. Diversity policies are complex and usually involve finances, perceptions of justice, fairness, and risk taking. It is the nuanced experiences of a multicultural workforce of multiracial citizens or honored strangers that will determine the future of many organizations around the world.

Honored Strangers Instruction Sheet for Group A

Immigrants

Your task is to develop scenarios of the immigrant experience based on your own or others' experiences. *You are to consider yourself as an immigrant to this country.* Your group will have thirty minutes for discussion of how this feels and what would be involved in becoming inculturated into your present workforce if you were an "outsider." You will make a five-minute presentation to all the participants based on a summary of your discussion.

Please share your experiences and discuss the following:

1. Two incidents you recall from your own experience with reference to immigrants and the world of work. If you share your own personal experience or that of significant others whom you know, the quality of the discussion is likely to be enhanced. (You may choose to discuss initial entry into the workforce, staying in the workforce, or interactions with colleagues.)

2. Two questions you would want to ask, but would be hesitant to ask, as an immigrant to your workplace.

3. What would your dream experience be for immigrants in the world of work?

Honored Strangers Instruction Sheet for Group B

Host Country Member/Immigrant

Your task is to develop scenarios of the immigrant experience based on your own experiences. *You are a member of the host country. You yourself were an immigrant some years ago, but are now a member of the host country and the mainstream at work.* Your group will have thirty minutes for discussion. You will make a five-minute presentation to all the participants based on a summary of your discussion.

Please share your own experiences as an immigrant in the fairly recent past and discuss the following:

1. Two incidents that stand out in your mind, with reference to immigrants and their integration into the workforce. If you can share your own personal experiences or that of significant others whom you know, the quality of the discussion is likely to be enhanced. (You may choose to discuss initial entry into the workforce, staying in the workforce, or interactions with colleagues.)

2. Two questions you would want to ask as a person who is both a member of the host country mainstream and who has recent ties to your home country.

3. What would your dream experience be for host country individuals as they interact with immigrants in the world of work?

Honored Strangers Instruction Sheet for Group C

Host Country Member/Native

Your task is to develop scenarios of the immigrant experience based on your own experiences. *You are to consider yourself as a native-born member of the host country majority culture.* Your group will have thirty minutes for discussion. You will make a five-minute presentation to all the participants based on a summary of your discussion.

Share your experiences and discuss the following:

1. Describe two incidents that stand out in your mind when you as a native interacted with immigrants to your country at work. Share your own personal experiences or those of significant others whom you know in order to enhance the discussion. (You may choose to discuss an your observations about an immigrant's initial entry into the workforce, staying in the workforce, or interactions with colleagues.)

2. List two questions you might ask as a host country native.

3. What would your dream experience be for host country individuals as they interact with immigrants in the world of work?

Honored Strangers Bibliography

Baker, S. (2002, August 26). The coming battle for immigrants. *Business Week,* pp. 86–87.

Berry, J. (1990). Psychology of acculturation: Understanding individuals moving between cultures. In R.W. Brislin (Ed.), *Applied cross-cultural psychology* (pp. 232–253). Newbury Park, CA: Sage.

Chen, C.C., & Eastman, W. (1997). Toward a civic culture for multicultural organizations. *Journal of Applied Behavioral Science, 33,* 454–470.

Cox, T.H., Jr., & Beale, R.L. (1997). *Developing competency to manage diversity.* San Francisco, CA: Jossey-Bass.

Ferraro, G.P. (1998). *The cultural dimensions of international business.* Upper Saddle River, NJ: Prentice Hall.

Gabriel, Y. (2003). Your home, my exile: Boundaries and "otherness" in antiquity and now. *Organization Studies, 24*(4), 619–632.

Hofstede, G. (1997). *Cultures and organizations: Software of the mind.* New York: McGraw-Hill.

Kolman, L., Noorderhaven, N.G., Hofstede, G., & Dienes, E. (2003). Cross-cultural differences in central Europe. *Journal of Managerial Psychology, 18*(1), 76–88.

McLeod, P.L., Lobel, S.A., & Cox, T., Jr. (1996). Ethnic diversity and creativity in small groups. *Small Group Research, 27,* 248–264.

Patrickson, M., & O'Brien, P. (Eds.). (2001). *Managing diversity.* Queensland, Australia: John Wiley & Sons.

Pio, E. (2004). Harder for us, easier for them: Work experiences of first generation immigrant women and their daughters. *International Journal of Diversity in Organizations, Communities and Nations.*

Pio, E. (2004). Indian women immigrants in New Zealand. *EEO Diversity Information & Research.* www.eeotrust.org.nz

Pio, E. (2005). Rich traditions: Managing diversity. *The 2005 Annual: Training.* San Francisco, CA: Pfeiffer.

Schwartz, S.H. (1999). A theory of cultural values and some implications for work. *Applied Psychology: An International Review, 48(1),* 23–47.

Sims, R.H., & Schraeder, M. (2004). An examination of salient factors affecting expatriate culture shock. *Journal of Business and Management, 10(1),* 73–87.

Stockdale, M., & Crosby, F.J. (Eds.). (2004). *The psychology and management of workplace diversity.* Oxford: Blackwell Publishers.

Taylor, R. (2003). Hardship at home/Hardship abroad: The migration "system" doesn't work. *UN Chronicle Online edition.* www.un.org/Pubs/chronicle/2003/issue1/0103p55.html

Trompenaars, F. (1993). *Riding the waves of culture.* London: The Economist Books.

Zanoni, P., & Janssens, M. (2003). Deconstructing difference: The rhetoric of human resource managers' diversity discourses. *Organization Studies, 25(1),* 55–74.

Windows
Demonstrating Group Competencies

Activity Summary

A project assignment that strengthens competencies in organization-specific areas as teams decorate a window for a special occasion or celebration.

Goals

- To help managers identify competencies in need of improvement from an organizational standpoint.

- To assist teams or department groups to consciously apply the identified competencies while decorating a window that also depicts the competencies and keeps the spirit of a special occasion.

- To enhance teamwork through reaching a common goal in a semi-competitive environment.

Group Size

The management group as well as several teams/groups of 4 to 10 persons from the same organization.

Time Required

Over a period of 1 to 2 weeks:

- 1 hour for a meeting with management.

- 30 minutes to meet with teams.

- 2 to 4 hours per team over about 10 days.

- 15 minutes per team for window presentations and judging.

- 20-minute award presentation and wrap-up discussion.

Materials

- Copies of typed instructions from the management meeting, including definitions of competencies, prepared by the facilitator.

- $30, or whatever is determined to be an adequate supply budget, for each team.

- Markers to be shared by management group or a sheet of colored sticky dots for each manager.

- Copies of the Windows Evaluation Form and Windows Sample Interview Questions for the judges.

- Flip chart and markers.

- Masking tape.

- Prizes

Physical Setting

A room large enough for each of the formal meetings. Glass windows (or doors) that can be decorated with non-permanent materials for a few weeks (large posters or flip charts can be used if necessary).

Facilitating Risk Rating

Moderate.

Process

1. Meet with the management team of the organization. Introduce the session by explaining that they are going to identify competencies that, if strengthened, would lead to a stronger organization.

2. Help them start to think by asking: "What are the competencies that you possess as a group that are serving you well?" If responses are slow in coming, follow with "What do you do well in this organization and why?" Record their responses on a flip chart. Be prepared to identify one or two characteristics that you, the facilitator, feel are strengths of the organization or group (e.g.,

a sense of urgency, excellent problem solving skills, good customer retention). List these and post the sheet.
(10 minutes.)

3. Next ask: "What challenges are you facing as an organization, such as changes in the business environment, competition, employee motivation or training, finding job candidates, and so forth?" List these and post the sheet.
(20 minutes.)

4. Finally, ask: "Bearing in mind the challenges you have identified and your current strengths, what skills, attitudes, or knowledge are key for you to develop within this organization for continued success?" List these and post the sheet.
(20 minutes.)

5. Give each of the managers a felt-tipped marker or sheet of sticky dots and ask them to place dots by the three (or more if desired) competencies they feel are most vital for the organization to develop right now and into the future. Use the nominal group technique to hone the list to the top four to six competencies (for example, effective communication, adapting to change, creativity, and understanding different roles in the organization).

6. Ask the management team whether there is any other information that would benefit management to have from the employees. For example, would they like to know what employees would find most useful from a new information system? If so, employees can be asked to create a "wish list." Explain that groups of employees will create "windows" that illustrate the organizational competencies from their own point of view. Answer any questions the managers have.

7. Have the management team determine the following:

   • A supply budget for the process.

   • When they will judge the "windows" (7 to 10 days later).

   • Who will be on the judging team (ask them to agree on three people).

   • What the prize will be for the winning team. (Alternatively, the management team can be prepared to award each team a prize if they feel they are deserving. Prizes need not be large, nor need they be material. A gift of time off is always appreciated, for example.)

   • Whether the prize(s) will be announced ahead of time or at the conclusion of the judging.

- Which member(s) of the management team will accompany the facilitator to deliver the assignment to the teams/groups.

- Date/time for the award presentation and activity wrap-up.
(10 minutes.)

8. As a follow-up, give typed copies of the competencies determined to be the most critical and the Windows Evaluation Form to all members of the management team.

9. In conjunction with the management team (if there is time) draft one or two questions per competency that may be used during the window judging. For example, if creativity is a desired competency, a question might be: "What roadblocks did your team encounter when creating your window? How did you work around them?" If effective communication is a competency, you might ask: "How did you gather ideas and input from the entire group?" (See Windows Sample Interview Questions.)

10. At the date agreed on, in the company of at least one member of the management group (more, if desired), hold a session with members of intact work teams within the organization.

11. Introduce the session by explaining that a different type of learning process will be incorporated into making the facility more festive for the occasion (pick an occasion) or to celebrate a special company or team accomplishment (as determined by management).

12. Explain that the management team has gone through a process to identify what is going well currently in the organization. Post the list and explain what the items mean.

13. Let the participants know that the management team has identified some other areas that, if "buffed up," could help to take the organization to an even higher level of performance.

14. Tell them that each team/department has been assigned to decorate a "window" for the occasion. Give them the date by which the work is to be completed and any other time-line details or project constraints (e.g., materials that may not be used).

15. Give them the list of competencies that are to be explored and strengthened. (It is possible to give different teams different lists.) Ask the participants to contribute to a definition of each of the competencies. (You may wish to have them work in small groups to do this.) Record their responses on a flip chart.

Let them know when you will provide the team/department leaders with a summary of what they have said.

(15 minutes.)

16. If the management team identified any additional deliverables, provide the teams/departments with this information also.

17. Give each team some money for supplies and a work space on which to post their "window." Convey your excitement about the project and your interest in seeing the results. Be specific about the expected results and deadlines. Mention that ALL members of a team must contribute to the final result. (If desired, a manager may speak with the group at this point.) Answer any questions and wish the teams luck.

18. On the designated date for judging and wrap-up, bring everyone together again and give each team 10 minutes to do the following:

    • Explain their window and show how the competencies from their list were incorporated into the window theme.

    • Describe how the competencies were utilized in the process of creating the window.

    (15 minutes.)

19. During each presentation, management judges should give full attention to the presenters for cues that the group utilized the competencies and have a good understanding of what each one means.

20. Give the judges an opportunity to ask questions of the teams to further understand how the competencies were used in the process. It will become apparent that the judging itself is part of the process to cement the commitment to deepening the competencies both within the teams/departments and among the judges themselves. (See the sample interview questions.)

21. Announce the order in which the windows will be judged. Allow about 15 minutes per window in order to conclude the scoring process. Be sure each judge has a copy of the Evaluation Form and encourage judges to comment to members of the teams and to give each team appreciation as they go along.

22. After all windows have been reviewed, reconvene the teams and ask a few follow-up questions:

    • How can you use the learning from the experience of decorating the windows together as we go forward?

- What surprised you most about this experience?

- What did the project help you learn about your teammates?

23. Announce the winner(s) and present the prizes. The leaders of the organization may take this opportunity to

- Share their gratitude for the engagement of the group.

- Highlight the key learning for both management and employees.

- Point out how the competencies will be vital to the organization in the coming year and beyond.

- Provide commentary that individuals benefit by strengthening these competencies, not just at work, but also in their communities and at home.

Variations

- Have the groups decorate a door or a package instead of a window.

- Have the competency discussions with the teams rather than with the management team.

- Use a theme for the windows that is very specific to the organization, such as a merger or acquisition or significant process change.

Submitted by Beverly J. Bitterman.

Beverly J. Bitterman, *owner of Beverly Bitterman and Associates, is a life and business coach and team developer. She is an effective facilitator who creates environments in which groups are comfortable communicating about issues, uncovering and removing barriers to high performance, and taking concrete action to move forward on projects. Ms. Bitterman teaches communication skills for the University of South Florida Continuing Education Department and has held several offices for the Nashville, Tennessee, chapter of ASTD.*

Windows Evaluation Form

1 = Some competency observed	2 = Working knowledge of the competency	3 = Understands interrelationship of the competency and carry over to other roles	4 = Master, capable of teaching/mentoring others in this competency

Team/Group Name: _____

Evaluator: _____

Points	Competency	Comments

_____ Total Points

Windows Sample Interview Questions

Awareness of each team or department's role and how they will be impacted by the software change.

- What are the positive benefits you see coming from the software for your team or department?

Effective Communication

- How did you gather ideas and input from the group for your window design?

- How did you decide between two or more options for your design?

Different Parts Working Together

- How did you divide up the work?

- What unique skills were demonstrated?

Adapting to Change

- What skills are important to be good at handling change?

- What do you do to help each other adapt to change?

Project Management

- How did you organize the tasks to be done?

- How did you keep track of who was doing what?

- Who called and managed the meetings?

Creativity

- What roadblocks did you encounter in the process? How did you work around them?

Team Spirit

- How does your team define team spirit? How is that shown in your window?

Trust ARCH
Building Team Support

Activity Summary

A team-building activity that allows participants to identify ways to increase trust among group members.

Goals

- To discuss actions and behaviors that create trust and undermine trust in groups.

- To identify characteristics that are important to building trust.

- To identify current and future actions that will increase trust in relationships.

Group Size

Several groups of 4 to 6 people from the same organization.

Time Required

Approximately 90 minutes.

Materials

- One copy of the Trust ARCH Handout for each participant.

- One copy of the Trust ARCH Worksheet for each participant.

- One copy of the Trust ARCH: What You Can Say handout for each participant.

- One copy of the Trust ARCH Action Planning Sheet for each participant.

- A pen or pencil for each participant.

- A flip chart and felt-tipped marker for each group.

- Masking tape.

Physical Setting

A room large enough for participants to work in groups without disturbing one another. Tables for groups to meet and record responses on worksheets and flip charts. Wall space is required for posting flip-chart sheets.

Facilitating Risk Rating

Moderate to high, depending on the relationships among participants.

Process

1. Introduce the session by stating that trust is an important element of effectiveness for groups and individuals who work together.

2. Ask the participants why trust is important. Discuss their responses for about 5 minutes. You may also record their responses on a flip chart and post it on the wall.
   (5 minutes.)

3. Ask participants how they would define trust. Discuss their responses and record them on a flip-chart page and post it on the wall.

4. Distribute a copy of the Trust ARCH Handout to each participant. Introduce the handout by discussing the following key points:

   - As we have discussed, trust is a building block for communication and effectiveness between individuals and within groups.

   - Architecturally, an *ARCH* is a type of opening that withstands pressure and is stronger than a square or rectangular opening. Therefore, an ARCH can be a metaphor for a relationship that is strong and withstands pressure. The ARCH is also an acronym for four essential elements of trust, as described on the handout.
   (5 minutes.)

5. Read the Trust ARCH Handout to the group and ask participants for a work-related example for each element.
   (10 minutes).

6. Distribute one Trust ARCH Worksheet to each participant, along with a pen or pencil. Read the directions to participants. Divide participants into groups of 4 to 6 individuals, preferably those who work together. Give each group a flip-chart page and marker. Ask each group to discuss the four elements of the Trust ARCH and to list four specific examples from their work groups that create trust and four that undermine trust.
    (10 minutes.)

7. Have each group post its flip-chart page of trust behaviors and have a representative read the group's list to the rest of the participants.
    (10 minutes.)

8. Discuss with the groups what trust-building behaviors are important to add to their interactions with each other. Discuss behaviors that undermine trust that they can agree to stop. Capture important agreements on flip-chart pages.
    (10 minutes.)

9. Ask participants how they might approach someone about a behavior that is undermining trust. Ask them what they might say to the person. Distribute a copy of Trust ARCH: What You Can Say to each participant. Ask participants to review the handout and identify what phrases they might be comfortable using with one another. Identify other phrases that might be added to the list.
    (10 minutes.)

10. Distribute a copy of the Trust ARCH Action Planning Sheet to each participant. Give participants 5 minutes to complete the worksheet. Remind them to pay particular attention to what they can do in the future to build trust within their work teams.

11. Depending on the size of the group, either conduct a round robin asking participants to report actions they will commit to doing, or have participants share their commitments within their small groups.
    (10 to 15 minutes.)

12. Lead a concluding discussion of the importance of honoring trust and building commitments; the importance of participants openly asking for what they need from each other; and the importance of communicating about actions that undermine trust. Consider asking the following questions:

    • What have you learned about the rule of trust in your work group?

    • How will you follow through on the commitments you made today?

- What do you need from one another to be able to meet these commitments?

- Where else can you apply what we have talked about today?
  (10 minutes.)

———————

Submitted by Mary B. Wacker.

Mary B. Wacker *focuses on professional coaching, business performance systems, and organizational change. Her company works with profit and not-for-profit businesses to develop high performance teams, leadership, and service systems. An accomplished international speaker, Ms. Wacker has written numerous training kits and programs cited in business publications. She is co-author of* Stories Trainers Tell: 55 Ready-to-Use Stories to Make Training Stick *(Pfeiffer, 2003) and a past president of the Southeastern Wisconsin Chapter of ASTD.*

The Trust ARCH Handout

Building effective teams requires that you create relationships based on trust. Four behaviors required to support the Trust ARCH, representing relationships based on trust, are

ADAPTABLE—to be flexible in your approach toward others. This requires an awareness of and appreciation for individual differences and non-judgmental acceptance of other people and situations. It might be expressed in the following way: "I communicate and act in ways that meet your needs."

RELIABLE—consistent follow-through on commitments and promises. This requires "owning" and communicating one's expectations to others, telling people what you will do, and then doing it. It might be expressed as: "I do what I say I'll do."

COMPETENT—effective technical and interpersonal skills. This requires the ability to act on something by using appropriate resources and problem-solving skills. It could be expressed as: "I know what to do."

HONEST—to inspire believability. Requires the ability to share information and be direct while still maintaining confidentiality when appropriate. This could be expressed as follows: "I tell it like it is."

Trust Arch Worksheet

Group Activity

From your own experiences, identify several examples of behaviors that CREATE TRUST in the workplace and several behaviors that UNDERMINE TRUST in the workplace. Be specific. For example, rather than say something like "Respect each other," list several specific ways RESPECT can be demonstrated through behaviors, such as "Critique ideas but don't criticize people."

Creates Trust	Undermines Trust

Trust ARCH: What You Can Say

Here are some ideas on how to begin a conversation to resolve a problem and increase trust between you and another person. Remember that your tone of voice and non-verbal behavior are also important in creating a climate that supports open, honest communication.

"I'd like to check out something with you. In our meeting I thought. . . . How did you see it?"

"This isn't working very well for me. How is it working for you?"

"I'd like to take a risk and tell you how I felt about. . . ."

"I'm uncomfortable with what is happening right now."

"What's most important to you in this situation? Here is what's important to me about it."

"How can we do this in a way that meets your needs? Is there a way we can meet *both* our needs?"

"What do you need right now?"

"Is this your understanding of what we agreed to do?"

"What do we want to do next time to resolve this problem?"

Trust ARCH Action Planning Sheet

	What I Do Now	What I'll Do in the Future
Adaptable		
Reliable		
Competent		
Honest		

The Team Circle
Moving from Conflict to Harmony

Activity Summary

Participants will have the opportunity to resolve real-life conflict scenarios utilizing the existing strengths of the team members.

Goals

- To gain an understanding of how conflict among individual team members affects the entire team.

- To understand how team members can overcome obstacles by using the strengths present on the team.

Group Size

8 to 10 participants who are currently working together on a team.

Time Required

35 to 45 minutes for activity and 15 minutes for pre-work.

Materials

- Copies of The Team Circle Survey for all participants.

- A copy of the Sample Start, Obstacle, and Strength Card Content for the facilitator.

- A long piece of string to make a circle on the floor (6 feet in diameter).

- The Team Circle Harmony Board drawn on a flip-chart easel (See Figure 1).

- Yellow Post-it® Obstacle Cards prepared in advance by the facilitator.

- Blue Post-it Strength Cards prepared in advance by the facilitator.

- Pink Post-it Notes to use as wild cards.

- The Team Circle Model handout for all participants.

- Flip chart and felt-tipped markers.

- Three 3 x 5 index cards.

Physical Setting

Room with a large open space to accommodate a large circle on the floor. An easel or wall space is necessary to display The Team Circle Harmony Board.

Facilitating Risk Rating

High.

Preparation

1. Two to three weeks in advance of the session, send The Team Circle Survey to team members electronically or in paper format. Tell participants it will take approximately 15 minutes to complete. Give them a deadline for returning the survey.

2. Compile the results of the survey and review the strengths and obstacles that are listed.

3. Create a "strength" card for each strength, one each on a blue Post-it Note. There must be one for each participant; if there are not enough due to duplication, you can create "wild cards" on pink Post-it Notes, without attributing a strength to the card. These will be created later by the team.

4. Create an "obstacle" card for each obstacle gathered from the survey. Again, create one for each participant, this time using yellow Post-it Notes. For obstacles, print a one- or two-sentence description of the obstacle as described.

5. Create a succinct statement to start the activity and to unite the team members and get them to move into the circle you will create on the floor. This statement can reference this activity or a prior team-building session, or can be any statement that unites the team.

6. Create a Team Circle Harmony Board on a flip-chart sheet. (See Figure 1.)

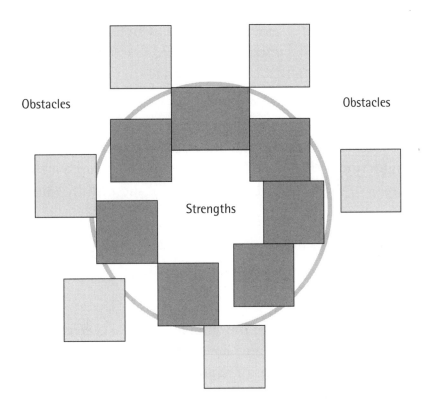

Obstacles

Obstacles

Strengths

Figure 1.   Team Circle Harmony Board

Process

1.   Just prior to the start of your session, place the string on the floor in the shape of a large circle and post the Harmony Board.

2.   Ask team members to stand on the outside of the circle, spread around the perimeter.

3.   Give each person one obstacle card and one strength card.

4.   Read your "Start" statement to move the group into the circle. Once you have read the card, the entire team should step into the circle, signifying a team in harmony.

5.   Choose a team member at random to read the scenario on his or her obstacle card aloud and then step back outside the circle. Tell the participant to decide how far out of the circle he or she want to stand based on the magnitude of the obstacle. Tell the person that he or she cannot move back into the circle until the obstacle has been addressed and resolved.

6.   The remaining team members should work together to find a way to resolve the conflict by using just ONE of their strength cards. (The strength card that

is outside the circle cannot be used.) Tell them that they may use "wild cards" to represent any strength the team would like to use to resolve the conflict. These would be strengths not mentioned on the survey or by you. If they wish to create a wild card, give them a pink Post-it and ask them to write the strength on it.

7. Tell the team member outside the circle to attach both the obstacle and the strength card to the Team Harmony Board and step back inside the circle when he or she feels the conflict has been successfully resolved.

8. Facilitate the process and interact with all participants on the outside and the inside of the circle to ensure that each conflict is resolved.

9. Once a team member is back inside the circle, ask for another volunteer to share another obstacle card.

10. Continue play until all of the strength and obstacle cards have been used and are posted on The Team Circle Harmony Board. Encourage participants to come up with strengths previously unrecognized by team members, that is, to create a lot of wild cards.
    (20 to 30 minutes.)

11. Ask the participants to return to their seats and lead a concluding discussion using the following questions. You may wish to note their answers on a flip chart.

    * How did you feel when you were on the inside of the circle?

    * How did you feel when you were on the outside of the circle?

    * What conflicts did you observe internally among the team members?

    * What did you observe that could be applied to your team back on the job?

12. Conclude by sharing that the strengths and obstacles were taken directly from the survey pre-work. Stress that the team was able to solve all of their obstacles using the strengths present on the team.

13. Share The Team Circle Model with the team and discuss using the visual model as a checkpoint for the team:

    * Is this team working inside the circle? *Harmony*

    * Are there members outside the circle? *Conflict*

Submitted by Bridget A. O'Brien

Bridget A. O'Brien *has been working in the field of training and development for over ten years. Her career began at Salomon Brothers in New York City in corporate training, designing and delivering training for proprietary software programs. The last four years, she has been working in organization development at Merck & Company, developing and facilitating team-building and leadership programs. Ms. O'Brien is currently completing her M.S. in organizational development and psychology at St. Joseph's University in Philadelphia.*

The Team Circle Survey

Instructions: Please complete the following survey and return it by: _____

1. Length of time as a member on your current team:

    ☐ 3 months or fewer   ☐ 4 to 6 months

    ☐ 6 to 11 months   ☐ 1 year or more

2. Indicate the number of times you have held the role of a team leader:

    ☐ 0   ☐ 1   ☐ 2   ☐ 3   ☐ 4+

3. Have you had any formal training in conflict resolution or problem solving?

    ☐ No   ☐ Yes.   Please specify the course or activity:

4. In your experience as a team member, please describe how conflict has been approached on your teams (be specific):

5. What do you see as your strengths when dealing with conflict among team members?

6. What do you see as your challenges when dealing with conflict among team members?

7. Do you feel a conflict-resolution/problem-solving workshop would be help-ful for your team at some point during the life of the team?

☐ No ☐ Yes. Please specify why you believe this:

8. Please list specific topics that should be included in a conflict-resolution/problem-solving workshop for your team:

9. What are some obstacles your team often encounters in its work?

10. What are some strengths members bring to your team?

11. Additional comments or suggestions:

The Team Circle Sample Start, Obstacle, and Strength Card Content

Sample Start Card

Team attends Kick-Off Meeting and learns valuable personal information about the individual members of the team.

Sample Situations and Resulting Obstacle Cards

(Fred's functional role is consistently pulling him away from the focus of the team.) Functional role conflicts within team.

(Isabel never sends the team minutes out on time and has not explained her behavior.) Identifying the source/motives of conflict.

(Juliet is consistently late for team meetings and the rest of the team is getting frustrated because the issue has not been addressed.) Not dealing with conflict immediately.

(The team has agreed to a December 1 deliverable. John doesn't think the deadline is realistic, but he is afraid to say anything because he doesn't want to rock the boat.) Setting realistic deadlines.

(Emma finds some of Riley's "humorous" comments to be personally offensive and doesn't know how to approach him to discuss the issue.) Lack of experience dealing with conflict.

(Isaac has personal commitments after work several days a week and cannot attend meetings scheduled after 3 p.m.) Work/life balance.

(Fred's functional manager has directed him to go against a team decision.) Driven by management instead of the team.

(Kevin is a hard worker and contributes a great deal to the team; however, he is extremely disorganized. Marta, the team leader, isn't sure if she should mention this to him or not.) Knowing what to let go and what to follow up.

Sample Strength Cards

Good communication skills

Ability to see all points of view and remain impartial

Good sense of humor

Ability to listen to others

Open-minded

Good working relationships outside the team

Diplomatic—approach the situation logically and rationally

The Team Circle Model

Conflict

Harmony

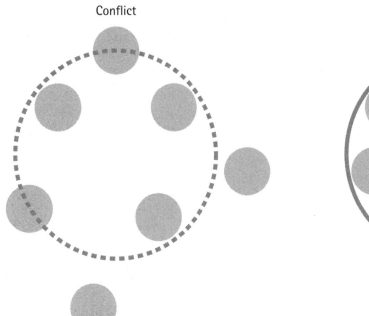
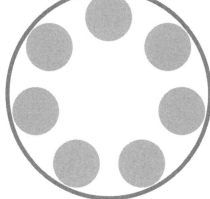

Beyond I, Me, and My
Honoring Separate Realities

Activity Summary

A poem-based small group discussion that allows participants to explore relationship dynamics created by divisive, conflict-producing behaviors versus relationship-sustaining behaviors and the resulting impacts on individual and organization success.

Goals

- To understand that each person "sees" and interprets situations differently, thereby creating individual realities.

- To identify behaviors that help individuals rise above rigid, one-best-way positions.

- To achieve inclusive solutions that sustain and nurture relationships, even in times of disagreement.

Group Size

Several groups of 5 or 7 participants.

Time Required

45 minutes.

Materials

- Beyond I, Me, and My Discussion Directions for each participant.

- Beyond I, Me, and My: "Green, Not Blue" for each participant.

- Beyond I, Me, and My Worksheet for each participant.

- Beyond I, Me, and My: Acknowledging Separate Realities for each participant.

- Paper and pencil for each participant.

- Timer or stop watch.

- Index card with "5 minutes" written in black felt-tip marker.

- Energy chime, whistle, or bell.

- Flip chart paper and felt-tip markers.

- Masking tape.

Physical Setting

Round tables with enough room between them so that groups do not disturb one another. Wall space to post charts.

Facilitating Risk Rating

Low.

Process

1. When participants are in groups of 5 to 7 at tables, introduce the concept of separate realities by saying that each person "sees" and interprets situations/relationships/environments differently, based on individual experiences, beliefs, and values. Explain that these interpretations create individual realities or what is called a "separate" reality.

2. Illustrate the concept of separate realities by drawing the following on the flip chart: in the lower left-hand corner, draw a circle. Label the circle "A" and say to the group that the circle represents Person A. Next, draw a square around the circle and say Person A's perspective of what is is illustrated by the square around the circle. The square represents Person A's perception of reality. Next, draw another circle in the lower right-hand corner directly across from Circle A. Label the circle "B" and say to the group that the circle represents Person B. Say that this person is a co-worker (or family member) who works (or lives) in the same environment. Draw a triangle around this circle and say that Person B's perspective of what is is illustrated by the triangle. Emphasize that Person A and Person B are viewing the same situation, yet each has a different perception of what is—or a separate reality.

3. Distribute to each participant a set of the Discussion Directions, the "Green, Not Blue" poem, and the Worksheet and a pen or pencil and tell them they will explore the concept of separate realities through small group discussion. Say that the activity is designed to illustrate how separate realities create the dynamics of human relationships.

4. Direct participants' attention to the Beyond I, Me, and My Discussion Directions. Tell the participants that you will walk them through the directions for the three handouts in order and that they are not to proceed until you have finished reading.

5. Read aloud the directions to each handout while they follow along. First read the Discussion Directions and then draw participants' attention to the "Green, Not Blue" poem by Sue Pettit and the I, Me, and My Worksheet.

6. Tell participants that they will prepare group reports at the end of the activity representing each group's responses to the third set of questions on the Worksheet.

    (10 minutes.)

7. Tell the participants they have 20 minutes to complete the entire activity using all three handouts and that you will walk among the groups with a card indicating when they have 5 minutes remaining. When time is up, you will call their attention back to the large group by ringing a chime [whistle or bell]. Demonstrate the sound of the chime [whistle or bell].

8. Ask whether there are any questions. Respond to any questions. Signal groups to begin.

9. Set a timer for 20 minutes, or use a stop watch. Circulate among the groups to monitor progress.

10. Watch the time. When 15 minutes have elapsed, inform groups they have 5 minutes left by walking around and showing the card to group leaders. Be sure to make eye contact with each small group leader so you know he or she is aware of the time.

11. When 20 minutes have elapsed, sound the energy chime [whistle or bell] to indicate that time is up.

    (20 minutes.)

12. Ask for a volunteer to come to the front and serve as a recorder while group facilitators report responses for the third set of questions. Ask the recorder to list the various groups' input on the flip chart.

13. Instruct the group facilitators to share a group response only if that response has not been shared by another group. Emphasize that the purpose of the group reports is to gather all *unique* ideas generated by the groups.

14. Facilitate group reports until all the unique ideas to the third set of questions (questions 8 through 12) have been recorded.

15. Give participants copies of Beyond I, Me, and My: Acknowledging Separate Realities.

16. Explain to the participants that honoring separate realities is a way to move from "either/or" positions to "and/so" viewpoints. To honor someone's separate reality does not mean that you agree with the person. It's a way to demonstrate a willingness to acknowledge that each person is "right" and "telling the truth" according to the way he or she sees it. To honor separate realities eliminates the need to defend one's entrenched position and allows each person to see things from his or her own perspective.

17. Refer them back to the diagram of Person A and Person B on the flip chart. Draw an oval in the center of the chart near the top. Then connect Circle A to the oval by drawing a dotted straight line upward to the middle of the oval. Next, connect Circle B to the oval by drawing a dotted straight line upward to the same spot on the oval so the overall image is a large triangle.

18. Explain to participants that when we honor each person's perception of what is, an environment is created for us to *rise above* our individual perceptions and create a solution that honors both realities. To honor separate realities is to *go beyond I, me, and my.*

19. Ask whether there are any concluding comments or insights participants wish to share. Facilitate closure with these questions:

   • What insights did you have as a result of this activity?

   • How will you incorporate what you learned into your life?

   • How can you implement this knowledge in the workplace?
   (15 minutes.)

Variation

The third set of questions can be tailored to specific departments or groups, for example, sales, customer service, family, church, etc.

Reference

Pettit, S.S. (1987) *Coming home: A collection.* Fair Oaks, CA: Sunrise Press.

Submitted by Marilyn J. Sprague-Smith.

Marilyn J. Sprague-Smith, *M.Ed., is an award-winning consultant, author, professional speaker, trainer, and certified laughter leader. Through her company, Miracles & Magic, she partners with organizations that want to transform creativity and innovation into mission-driven results. Ms. Sprague-Smith is the 2003 recipient of the prestigious Larry Wilson Award, which is presented annually to an outstanding educator in a non-school-based setting by the University of Minnesota's College of Education and Human Development Alumni Society.*

Beyond I, Me, and My Discussion Directions

Instructions: Determine which member of your group has a birthday closest to today. This person will serve as group facilitator.

The group facilitator is to read the first paragraph of the poem aloud. Then individual members of the group read the next lines of the poem aloud, in turn. Continue the process until you reach the first STOP.

At that point, the "group facilitator" leads a group discussion of the first set of questions on the Beyond I, Me, and My Worksheet.

Next, return to the poem and continue reading it aloud, taking turns until you reach the next STOP. At that point, the group facilitator is to lead a discussion of the second set of questions on the worksheet.

Again, return to the poem and continue reading aloud until you reach the end of the poem. Now the group facilitator is to lead a discussion of the third set of questions on the worksheet, ensuring that each member of the group has an opportunity to respond. Your group will report your answers to these questions back to the large group. You have 20 minutes to complete the entire task.

Beyond I, Me, and My: "Green, Not Blue"

Sue Pettit

I was out for a walk
When I happened to meet
The woman next door—
She was new on our street.
She nodded her head,
I returned her a smile.
And I thought—
She seems nice.
We've a similar style.
The next day we met
I took over some flowers.
We hit it off well.
We talked several hours.
She told me of her life.
I told her of mine.
And I thought—
I do like her.
This new neighbor's fine.
Then one day in the yard—
it is shocking but true—
this new friend of mine
called my green grass blue.
She kept calling green blue
'til I got so upset
And I thought—
I don't like her.
I'm sorry we met.

STOP
Go to first set of questions on worksheet.

In everything else
We had seen eye to eye;
From the red of the rose
to the blue of the sky.
Now she disagreed firmly
with no hesitation.
And I thought—
I am right
and I'll get validation!
I called over Marie,
a real long-time friend.
I just had to give
this discussion an end.
"Marie," I said, "Tell her
that this grass is green!"
And I thought—
What a neighbor—
to make such a scene.
Marie looked at it closely,
Examined its hue.
She saw lots of my green—
not a hint of her blue.
So I nodded my head
and I folded my arms.
And I thought—
Whew, I'm right.
There's no cause for alarm.
But my neighbor just smiled
and she said, "It's ok.
I just happen to see
your green grass my own way."
She wouldn't admit
that she saw green all wrong.
So I thought—
With her outlook
our friend days are gone.

STOP
Go to second set of questions on
worksheet.

> I stopped going over
> to visit with her.
> What I saw and she saw
> just didn't concur.
> We couldn't be friends
> 'cause we didn't agree.
> For I thought—
> All my friends
> Have to see just like me.
> As the years passed me by
> lots of friends passed by too
> Over matters important—
> like green versus blue.
> Just one little difference

> could lead to a fight.
> 'Cause I thought—
> In my world,
> there is only one right.
> I'm much wiser now.
> I don't see the same way.
> My heart
> not my eyes
> looks upon each new day.
> When I look from my heart,
> friends are blessings to me.
> Without thought—
> There is room
> for all colors,
> I see.

STOP
Go to third set of questions on worksheet.

Source: Pettit, S.S. (1987) *Coming home: A collection.* Fair Oaks, CA: Sunrise Press. Most recently published by Sheridan Books, Inc. (2004). Reprinted by permission of Dr. William F. Pettit, M.D.

Beyond I, Me, and My Worksheet

Question Set 1

Group facilitator leads group discussion.

1. How did the poem's narrator meet her new neighbor?

2. What was her first impression of her new neighbor?

3. How did the narrator and her new neighbor get along right after they met?

4. What caused the narrator to be sorry she met her new neighbor?

Return to poem and read until you reach the next STOP.

Question Set 2

Group facilitator leads group discussion.

5. Why do you suppose the narrator and her neighbor responded the way they did?

6. How did the narrator attempt to prove she was "right"?

7. Why do you suppose she felt it was necessary to seek external validation?

8. In what way(s) did the narrator and her neighbor respond to Marie's viewpoint? Why do you suppose the narrator and her neighbor responded the way they did?

Return to the poem and read until you reach the next STOP.

Question Set 3

Group facilitator leads group discussion. (*Note:* Group reports will be made to the large group for group responses to these questions.)

9. How does the concept of separate realities relate to your daily activities/interactions at work?

10. In what ways do separate realities hinder successful outcomes in your work environment?

11. In what ways do separate realities nurture successful outcomes in your work environment?

12. What specific actions can you take to acknowledge separate realities in your work environment?

13. What specific benefits will you derive from being more aware of separate realities in your work environment?

Beyond I, Me, and My: Acknowledging Separate Realities

When we acknowledge separate realities, each of us is "right" and each of us is "telling the truth" as we see it!

When we acknowledge separate realities, we move from "either/or" positions—

"If you would just get your act together, everything would be just fine!"

to "and/so" viewpoints.

You're right!

Pass the Solution, Please
Brainstorming Suggestions

Activity Summary

A group brain-writing exercise to initiate opinions and feedback about a particular issue in a non-threatening, individualized way.

Goals

- To solicit opinions, feedback, and suggestions from group members about dealing with an issue or problem.

- To allow candid and anonymous comments and suggestions.

Group Size

An unlimited number of small groups with 5 to 8 members each.

Time Required

Approximately 15 minutes per round of writing. Allow 45 minutes for discussion of ideas received.

Materials

- A pen and a blank piece of paper or a piece of flip-chart sheet for each person.

Physical Setting

Conference room, ballroom, or any place with tables.

Facilitating Risk Rating

Moderate.

Process

1. Introduce the activity by forming groups of 5 to 8 seated at tables and asking participants to think of a problem or issue they would like suggestions for improving.

2. Have each person write a problem or issue he or she wants suggestions for handling at the *top* of a piece of paper—phrased in the form of a question.

3. Have participants pass their questions to the individuals to their right.

4. Ask these individuals to write their suggestions for a solution at the *bottom* of the page (NOT right under the question), fold the page up from the bottom just enough to hide their answers, and then pass the papers to the participants to their right.

5. This action continues until the piece of paper (all folded up *from the bottom* to hide each successive person's answers from the next) returns to its originator.

6. Once each person has his or her original question back, have everyone unfold their papers and read the four to seven possible solutions they received to the room at large. (If there are too many participants for everyone to share all ideas, re-form groups for discussion at tables.)

7. Give each person an opportunity to solicit more information from his or her group or clarify solutions that were offered through discussion and dialogue. *(10 minutes per table.)*

8. Ask for volunteers who would like to share their questions and some of the solutions offered. Use the following questions to lead a discussion.

    *   How helpful were the ideas you received?

    *   Will you be able to use some of the suggestions? Which ones? In what way?

    *   How will you implement the ideas you received?

    Be flexible with the time here, allowing enough time for meaningful answers.

Variation

Discussion can be held and action steps outlined later in the day or at a later time after participants have had time to think about the solutions offered or try some of them.

Submitted by Gail Hahn.

Gail Hahn, *MA, CSP, CPRP, CLL, is the CEO (Chief Energizing Officer) of Fun*cilitators and author of* Hit Any Key to Energize Your Life *as well as contributing author to over seventeen other books. She is an international keynote speaker, corporate trainer, and an award-winning team-building facilitator who is the only person in the world holding all four authentic certifications of Speaking Professional, Parks and Recreation Professional, Laugh Leader, and Strength Deployment Inventory® Facilitator.*

Empowerment
Ensuring the Basics Are in Place

Activity Summary

Multiple teams build structures from Lego® materials to uncover empowerment basics.

Goal

To explore how clarity of purpose, procedures, organization structure, organizational roles, and knowledge relate to empowerment.

Group Size

Any number of groups of 5 to 7.

Time Required

60 minutes.

Materials Required

- One Lego model set, such as a boat, plane, or car, for each team. Each set should have roughly 60 to 100 pieces. Note that the sets for teams 1 and 6 should be presorted by color and type.

- Random collections of the same number of Lego pieces for teams 3 and 4.

- One Empowerment Overview of Instruction Sheets (for the Facilitator).

- One of the six Empowerment Instruction Sheets for each team.

- Pictures of the model as assembled for Teams 1, 2, and 6.

- Step-by-step instructions (taken from the Lego set) for building the model for Teams 1 and 6. (Note that you may need to use the pictures provided rather than written instructions, as many Lego sets do not have written directions.)

Physical Setting

Room large enough to accommodate each team at a separate table and where teams will not overhear one another.

Facilitating Risk Rating

Moderate.

Process

1. Arrange participants into six or more subgroups of 5 to 7 members each.

2. Explain that each group has the task of creating a model using the materials provided.

3. Give a different Empowerment Instruction Sheet to members of each team. Give materials to teams according to the chart, and give leaders the appropriate instructions in an unobtrusive manner so it is not immediately clear that teams are operating on different terms.

4. Instruct teams to begin building their models on the basis of their instructions.

5. Move around the room and provide time updates to teams that have time limits in their instructions (all but Teams 4 and 6).
   (20 minutes.)

6. At the end of 20 minutes, instruct all teams to stop building their structures.

7. Begin the debriefing by discussing the construct of the exercise (varying instructions by team) and read the summary outlines of the six instruction sheets to the total group. Ask teams to raise their hands as you read the assumptions their team was operating under.
   (5 minutes.)

8. Debrief the exercise using the discussion questions below:

   - How did you go about organizing your efforts? What was empowering/disempowering about how you approached your project?

   - Which instructions were empowering/disempowering?

- How did the existence or lack of a clear definition of success impact your team's functioning?

- Were you committed to your task? Why or why not?

- What did you do to encourage and support one another?

- What specific factors of this exercise encouraged or discouraged how empowered you felt?

- What similarities are there between this exercise and how you operate in your organization?

- What can you take back to the workplace from this exercise to empower others?

(20 minutes.)

9. Have the five group leaders act as the "design review team" to select the winning model and award prizes. The design review team can use whatever criteria they wish to select the winner.
   (10 minutes.)

Trainer's Notes

- While some teams have a specific model-building set, other teams are free to build whatever they desire.

- Random collections of Legos should be used for Team 4, which has no specific instructions.

- You can also use observers and have them share during the discussion.

- If teams have questions during the exercise, refer them back to their instruction sheets.

Submitted by Chris W. Chen.

Chris W. Chen *is an OD manager with Sempra Energy and runs his own consulting business. He was a program manager at the Center for Creative Leadership and an adjunct professor at California State University, Long Beach. He's published four books:* Simply Spoken Leadership, New Supervisor Training, Coaching Training, *and* The Big Book of Six Sigma Training Games. *He's also published articles on a variety of human resource topics and been quoted by the* Washington Post *and* Chicago Tribune.

Empowerment Overview of Instruction Sheets

Team 1

    A. *Clarity of purpose:* Full, step-by-step instructions with a picture of the end state provided only to the leader.

    B. *Time:* 10-minute time allotment for design and 10 minutes for construction.

    C. *Incentives:* Prizes to team that completes its model correctly first.

    D. *Role definition:* Identify a team leader. Only the leader can see the instructions.

    E. *Process:* Provide materials pre-sorted by color/type.

Team 2

    A. *Clarity of purpose:* Picture of end state with no other instructions.

    B. *Time:* 10-minute time allotment for design and 10 minutes for construction.

    C. *Incentives:* No prizes mentioned.

    D. *Role definition:* Identify a team leader, who will be the timekeeper and the coordinator.

    E. *Process:* Provide materials unsorted.

Team 3

    A. *Clarity of purpose:* Build a simple structure.

    B. *Time:* 20 minutes for construction.

    C. *Incentives:* No prizes mentioned.

    D. *Role definition:* Identify a team leader, who will be the timekeeper and the coordinator.

    E. *Process:* Provide materials unsorted.

Team 4

    A. *Clarity of purpose:* Build a simple structure.

    B. *Time:* No time limits mentioned.

    C. *Incentives:* No prizes mentioned

    D. *Role Definition:* No assigned roles

    E. *Process:* Provide materials unsorted.

Team 5

A. *Clarity of purpose:* Picture of the end state with no other instructions.

B. *Time:* 20 minutes for construction.

C. *Incentives:* Prizes to team that complete their model correctly first.

D. *Role definition:* Identify a team leader, who will be the timekeeper and the coordinator.

E. *Process:* Provide materials unsorted.

Team 6

A. *Clarity of purpose:* Full, step-by-step instructions with a picture of the end state.

B. *Time:* No time limits mentioned.

C. *Incentives:* Prizes to team that complete their model correctly first.

D. *Role definition:* Identify a team leader, who will be the timekeeper and coordinator.

E. *Process:* Provide materials pre-sorted by color/type.

Team	Instructions	Time Limit	Incentives	Roles	Materials
1	step-by-step plus picture	10 + 10	prizes	team leader who is only one who may see instructions	presorted by color/type
2	picture of model only	10 + 10	no mention	team leader keeps time, coordinates	unsorted
3	unspecified structure	20	no mention	team leader keeps time, coordinates	unsorted
4	unspecified structure	no mention	no mention	no mention	unsorted
5	picture only	20	prizes	team leader keeps time, coordinates	unsorted
6	step-by-step plus picture	no mention	prizes	team leader coordinates	presorted by color/type

Empowerment Instructions for Team 1

Choose a leader for your team. He or she will obtain the instructions, a picture of the model you are to build, and a set of Lego blocks from the facilitator. ONLY your instructor may see the instructions and the picture. Your group will have 10 minutes to design and 10 minutes to build the structure. Prizes will be awarded to the team that completes its model correctly first.

Empowerment Instructions for Team 2

Choose a leader for your team. He or she will obtain a picture of the model you are to build and a set of Lego blocks from the facilitator. Your group will have 10 minutes to design and 10 minutes to build the structure. Your team leader will keep time and coordinate the process.

Empowerment Instructions for Team 3

Choose a leader for your team. He or she will keep time and coordinate your efforts during this activity. Your group will have 20 minutes to build a structure of some kind using the Lego blocks your facilitator will provide.

Empowerment Instructions for Team 4

Your group will build a structure using Lego blocks provided by the facilitator.

Empowerment Instructions for Team 5

Choose a leader for your team. He or she will obtain a picture of the model you are to build and a set of Lego blocks from the facilitator. Your group will have 20 minutes to design and build the structure. Prizes will be awarded to the team that completes its model correctly first.

Empowerment Instructions for Team 6

Choose a leader for your team. He or she will obtain the instructions, a picture of the model you are to build, and a set of Lego blocks from the facilitator. Your leader will coordinate the group's work. Prizes will be awarded to the team that completes its model correctly first.

Your Fantasy Work Team
Building a Perfect Team

Activity Summary

Participants are asked to imagine who would be on their fantasy work team (similar to thinking up a fantasy sports team).

Goals

- To help participants better understand the skills, abilities, and attitudes that would be ideal on their teams at work.

- To give participants insights for how the qualities desired for their fantasy team might be developed in their real teams at work.

- To create developmental goals for employees.

Group Size

Any size group of individuals who work together.

Time Required

40 to 50 minutes.

Materials

- One copy of the Your Fantasy Work Team Matrix for each participant.

- A pen or pencil for each participant.

Physical Setting

A room with enough seating space that participants can work independently and keep their answers private. Each participant should be comfortably seated and have a writing surface upon which to work.

Facilitating Risk Rating

Moderate.

Process

1. Introduce the activity by referencing the popularity of fantasy sports teams, which have become increasingly popular in recent years. Fantasy sports provide enthusiastic fans the opportunity to create the team of their dreams. These teams are made up of those players the fan believes would meet his or her every sports fantasy. The performance of these imaginary teams is measured by the actual results of the players when playing on their real teams to determine the fantasy contest winners. For example, a fan may pick players from a variety of professional football teams each week and then track their actual game performance on Sunday, combining these accomplishments as if they all actually played on the same team.

2. Ask participants to just imagine that they could create such a fantasy team at work. With this magnificent team, even the most difficult and challenging goals could be achieved. Nothing would be too difficult or impossible for these superstars. This dream team could propel them to a whole new level of performance in the future, one never even imagined in the past. Collectively, the team could accomplish objectives and goals that would become legendary in your organization.
   (5 minutes.)

3. Explain that in this activity, participants are going to take this fantasy to a new level. Ask participants to indulge this fantasy for at least a few minutes and think seriously about who would be on such a fantasy work team. After they have pondered this for a few minutes, explain that a few rules must be followed. Say: "Even your fantasies must have some rules!"

4. Explain the following rules to participants:

   - *Temporarily suspend disbelief*—don't let reality get in the way of your fantasy.

- *Think big*—as long as you are going to fantasize, you might as well make it great.

- *Look for a variety of qualities*—don't just pick players with the same skills or abilities. Think about the diversity you would need on your team.

- *Assume quick learning*—don't worry about players not knowing a particular job today, but assume that these skills could be quickly learned by that person.

5. Distribute copies of the Your Fantasy Work Team Matrix and pens or pencils to participants.

6. Review the instructions with participants before asking them to complete the Matrix.
   (20 to 30 minutes.)

7. After all participants have had enough time to complete the matrix, explain that now it's time to take fantasy to reality. Set the stage for this part of the exercise by asking participants what they think it would be like if they could actually assemble this group as a team. Once participants have had a chance to think about this, bring the group back to reality with a discussion about how unlikely it is that such a fantasy team would ever be assembled. More likely, the team that participants work with will be comprised of individuals who don't appear on their matrix. Such is life. But the real question is: "How can you help your actual work team function more like your fantasy team?"
   (5 minutes.)

8. Ask participants to once again look at the matrix they developed. Ask each person to think about how the individuals on their real work team could learn to achieve some or all of the same objectives they expected from their fantasy work team.

9. Ask participants to look at the list of skills that they hoped for on the fantasy team. Ask them the following questions:

- How can you help your actual team members develop the skills you need?

- What training, experiences, or developmental assignments could be provided that would move your team closer to having the skills your fantasy team possessed?

- Similarly, what strengths that you hoped would be part of your fantasy team could be developed in these individuals?

- How could you assist those with whom you currently work to make the contributions to the team that you desire?

- If you have the opportunity to hire additional members for your team, how can you ensure that you seek those attributes you said you would want on your fantasy team?

(10 minutes.)

10. Summarize the activity by asking participants to think about how the ideal can help one to better understand what can be done to develop the real. Say that fantasies can be helpful if we utilize them to help us improve our realities. Often identifying what we really want is the most important step toward actualization of our dreams. If we can first dream it, we will have a better chance of achieving our goals.

Submitted by Peter R. Garber.

Peter R. Garber *is currently manager of Equal Employment Opportunity at PPG Industries, Inc., Pittsburgh, Pennsylvania. He is author of seven books on a variety of business topics, including his most recent work,* Giving and Receiving Performance Feedback. *He is also a training specialist and consultant. Mr. Garber is a regular contributor to the* Annuals.

Your Fantasy Work Team Matrix

Instructions

1. Think of people who would be ideal members of your work team. List the individuals' names in the first column of the matrix. Don't worry about real-life limitations or realities, such as geographic restrictions, other commitments, or even qualifications. Just pick the people you believe—if all obstacles were removed—would comprise the ultimate work team.

2. Assign positions in the second column for each of your fantasy team members. Again, don't let such realities as availability, interest, certifications, openings, etc., get in the way of your fantasy. Just put those people you think, if given the optimum situation, would do the best job on your fantasy work team.

3. In the third column, list the skills that each person you selected would bring to your work team. Examples might include expertise in the field, technical knowledge, experience, etc.

4. List the strengths that each individual would bring to the team and position you assigned him or her. Strengths might be tenacity, creativity, diplomacy, dedication, loyalty, etc.

5. Last, list the contributions you believe each individual would bring to the team. Contributions might include creating a team spirit or camaraderie, positive attitude, knowledge, or imagination, to name a few.

Name	Position	Skills	Strengths	Contributions

Lights, Camera, Action!
Creating Team Commercials

Activity Summary

An interactive, creative opportunity for teams to share information about what they do with other teams within the department, division, or organization.

Goals

- To share information about the roles and responsibilities of different groups within a team, department, division, or organization.

- To build teamwork and communication skills.

Group Size

Two or more groups of 4 to 10 people from the same organization, with each group made up of individuals from the same team (department/work unit).

Time Required

1 to 1½ hours (depending on number of teams).

Materials

- Box filled with "props" available for teams to use. Props can include hats, capes, canes, stickers, towels, colorful paper, yarn, balloons, kazoos, cymbals, or a variety of dollar store items. The more unusual and playful, the better!

- One Lights, Camera, Action! Instruction Sheet for each team.

- (Optional) Clapboard.

- Flip chart and markers.

- Masking tape.

Physical Setting

A room large enough for the groups to work without disturbing each other. Round tables are recommended to facilitate discussion.

Facilitating Risk Rating

Moderate.

Process

1. Introduce the activity by explaining that it is amazing how often we work for the same division or company, but do not really understand what different parts of the organization do. Sometimes, this lack of understanding actually gets in the way of our productivity, and we end up making someone else's job harder without intending to. Ask the group for examples from their own experience of when they've seen this happen.
   (10 minutes.)

2. Ask everyone to get into the spirit of prime time TV, because they are about to create some commercials, designed to "sell" their team (division, work unit, etc.). Explain that the secret of a good commercial is two-fold: the concept of a memorable "sound bite" and the entertainment value.

3. Divide the participants into actual work teams of four to ten each. Explain that the goal of the activity is for each group to create a 2-minute commercial that is both informative and entertaining, which will clearly communicate their role and contribution to the division or organization as a whole. Read and post the following rules:

   - You may use any materials in the Prop Box, located in the front of the room, as well as any other "props" that you may find within the room.

   - Your entire team must participate in the presentation of your commercial.

4. Distribute one Lights, Camera, Action! Instruction Sheet to each team. Allow approximately 15 minutes for the teams to develop their commercials. Give a two-minute warning to teams.
   (20 minutes.)

5. Invite each team to present its commercial for the entire group. (For greater impact, it is fun to have an actual clapboard to use as you introduce each team's commercial.)

   (10 minutes.)

6. When all teams have presented their commercials, debrief using the following questions, capturing key information on a flip chart:

   • What have you learned that you didn't know before about the other teams in this division or organization?

   • How will you use this new information in the work *you* do?

   • What was the hardest part about creating your own commercial?

   • How did your team approach the design of the commercial?

   • What did you expect to hear that you did not hear?

   • How can we use what we have learned to help us work more productively together? What changes do we need to make as an organization?

   (20 minutes.)

Variations

   • Add the following challenge to the instructions: Include information in your commercial that will be a surprise to the rest of the group (i.e., a statistical piece of information; some trivia about your group; etc.).

   • Allow the group to vote for the "Most Popular Commercial" using specific criteria, such as entertainment value, new information shared, or most unusual presentation style.

   • Use the activity within a cross-functional team to create better understanding of roles and expectations.

Submitted by Cher Holton.

Cher Holton, *Ph.D., president of The Holton Consulting Group, Inc., is an Impact Consultant focusing on Bringing Harmony to Life with customers, among team members, and in life. She is one of fewer than two dozen professionals world-wide who have earned both the Certified Speaking Professional and Certified Management Consultant designations. She authored* The Manager's Short Course to a Long Career, Living at the Speed of Life: Staying in Control in a World Gone Bonkers!, *and* Crackerjack Choices: 200 of the Best Choices You Will Ever Make.

Lights, Camera, Action! Instruction Sheet

Goal

Your goal is to create a 2-minute commercial that is both informative and entertaining and that will clearly share your unit's role and what you do for this organization.

The Rules

- As a team, you are to create an entertaining and informative 2-minute commercial about the role of your unit.

- You may use any materials in the Prop Box or any other "props" you have that are already located in this room.

- Your entire team (Yes, that means EVERYONE) must participate in the presentation of your commercial.

- You will be expected to be ready to present your commercial to the rest of the group at: [fill in time given by your facilitator].

The Web We Weave
Closing the Team's Work

Activity Summary

To demonstrate the interrelationships and importance of each team member—particularly at the end of the team's work.

Goal

To acknowledge the work that each individual team member contributes to the team's success.

Group Size

5 or more people.

Time Required

10 to 20 minutes, depending on group size.

Materials

A ball of yarn.

Physical Setting

A space large enough for the group to gather (sit or stand) in a circle.

Facilitating Risk Rating

Moderate.

Process

1. As a way to bring closure to individual contributions to the team's success, ask the team to sit in a circle.

2. Hold a ball of yarn in your hand and begin the process by saying, "We all are important to this team's success and we couldn't have been successful without your individual contributions. So let's celebrate and thank our teammates. Here's how I suggest we proceed: I'll start by saying I would like to thank [Name] for [accomplishment]. For example, I'd like to thank [Larry] for [staying late one night, when I knew it wasn't convenient, to finish compiling the numbers for the team]."

3. Once you have thanked the person, wrap the yarn around your finger, and throw the ball to that person. Then the person thanks someone else, wraps the yarn around his or her finger, and throws the ball to the person being thanked, and so on.

4. After several passes, comment on how we weave a web of interconnectivity and dependence on each team member. (Yes, there is a risk that one or two team members didn't pull their weight, but usually the team will make sure they are included somehow, but the message does get sent in a subtle manner that they, in fact, did not pull their weight!)

5. Continue until everyone has been thanked for at least one contribution to the team's effort and/or the activity appears to slow down, but check with the team first. If they want to continue, do so.

6. When finished acknowledging the team's work, debrief the activity by asking the team to look at the web they weave. Say: "We are only as strong as all of us. And look at what happens when we aren't there to help each other."

7. Ask the team to take the yarn off their fingers. Comment on how the yarn has lost its beautiful shape and form! *Or* ask one team member to grab as much yarn as he or she can. See how one person can affect the balance of the team dynamic by taking the yarn.

Variation

For new teams, whoever catches the ball of yarn has to share a "fact" about him- or herself—either personal or work-related.

Submitted by Kristin J. Arnold.

Kristin J. Arnold, *CPF, CMC, CSP, helps corporations, government, and nonprofit organizations build high performance teams. She specializes in facilitating executives and their teams as well as training others to facilitate teams to higher levels of performance. An accomplished author as well as a featured columnist in the Daily Press, Ms. Arnold is regarded as an expert in process and team development. She graduated with high honors from the U.S. Coast Guard Academy and earned her MBA with an emphasis on marketing strategy from St. Mary's College in California.*

Towers
Preventing Business Failure

Activity Summary

Participants in this activity, acting as members of an organization's management team, will consider, discuss, and propose solutions to a variety of economic, customer, and employee issues and will experience how such issues can influence the success or failure of the business.

Goals

- To introduce participants to the three main categories of factors that influence business effectiveness and illustrate the complex relationships that exist among those factors.

- To illustrate the benefits of using teams to make decisions, solve problems, and address the types of issues that impact business success.

- To allow participants to identify individual/organizational factors and behaviors that contribute to or work against business achievement.

Group Size

Groups between 3 and 5 persons each. The number of groups is limited only by the number of Rainbow Jumbling Tower games purchased.

Time Required

70 to 80 minutes. In addition, the extent to which the activity is debriefed can add up to an additional hour.

Materials

Prepare the required materials in advance of the workshop.

- One Rainbow Jumbling Tower game (Item # 203T) per group. This game is manufactured by Cardinal Industries, Inc. 21–01 51st Avenue, Long Island City, NY 11101. Visit their website at www.cardinalgames.com. Games can be purchased either directly from the company or from assorted retail establishments, such as Wal-Mart, Target, or K-Mart. A sample tower is shown in the figure. (*Note:* The colors of the blocks in the rows should be mixed in advance of the workshop. The towers and color cubes should be kept in the canisters until it is time to begin the activity.)

- One set each of Towers Economic, Customer, and Employee Impact cards per group. (*Note:* These cards must be prepared in advance and may be customized to a specific business, organization, or industry. They are best printed on heavy 8.5 by 11-inch colored card stock (red, blue, and yellow, representing the colors of the blocks in the tower). (Lamination is optional.) It is helpful to place cards in a clear sealed plastic bag for storage.

- One Towers Rule Sheet per group.

Physical Setting

A room large enough for the groups to work at individual tables. Round tables work best, but the activity can be conducted on square or rectangular tables. Group members must be able to access all sides of the table.

Facilitating Risk Rating

Low.

Preparation

In advance of the activity, make sets of cards. In the case of the Economic Impact Cards, you must create cards pertinent to your organization's situation, typing them onto cards yourself. The Customer and Employee cards have been prepared for you and must be copied and cut out, although you may also add your own.

Process

1. Divide the participants into groups of between 3 to 5 individuals. Have each group gather around a table where a tower canister and cards have been placed in advance of the activity.

2. Instruct the participants to remove the towers from the canisters and separately shuffle each color of cards, placing them face down on the table.

3. Advise the participants that each tower represents their business and that they are managers of the business.

4. Introduce the activity by explaining that business success is influenced by many factors, which generally fall into three categories, *economic, customer,* and *employee.* Advise the participants that within their groups they will consider and discuss some of these issues.
   (10 minutes.)

5. Inform the participants that, as managers of the business, their job is to work with the other members of the management team to address issues that affect the business in such a way as to ensure the long-term viability and stability of the business (i.e., prevent the tower from falling down).

6. Advise the participants that this activity will allow them to experience how the types of issues that they face day-to-day can directly or indirectly influence the success or failure of an organization.

7. Distribute one copy of the Towers Rules Sheet to each group. Read the rules aloud and check for general understanding. Do not be too specific in providing detailed instructions. Some lack of clarification is effective in simulating a "real-world" experience for the participants.
   (10 minutes.)

8. Explain to the participants that the activity is not intended to be competitive; however, the activity will continue for approximately 20 minutes or until a business "falls."

9. The activity begins and members of the team take turns doing the following:

   • Throwing the colored cube.

   • Selecting a card from the three stacks as determined by the throw.

   • Reading the card aloud to the team.

   • Suggesting a solution or facilitating a brief discussion among the team regarding possible solutions to the issues. Once a general consensus among the group is reached about what to do, set the card aside and prepare to initiate action.

   • From the bottom half of the tower, identify a block that has the same color as the discarded card and cube.

   • Using one hand, remove the block from its current place in the tower and place it in a new location on top of the tower.

   • Continue the activity until time has expired or until the tower falls. *(25 minutes.)*

10. Give a 3-minute warning before calling time. Encourage teams to move quickly through the activity and not get bogged down on any one issue or discussion.

11. If a tower falls, the activity ends for that particular group, but should continue for the other groups until you call time.

12. Have participants return to their seats and lead a discussion about the activity by asking the following questions:

    • In what ways did the activity simulate life/reality within the business environment?

    • Was there any competition between your group and other groups as you tried to keep the towers from falling? If so, why do you think there was? The instructions clearly indicated that the activity was not competitive in nature.

    • How easy or difficult was it to reach consensus within your group regarding possible solutions to the issues. What types of things influenced your team's ability to reach consensus? (Consider things like organizational structure, culture, values, policies, procedures, and practices.)

    • What did you learn about the impact that economic, customer, and employee issues have on a business? Does one category carry a greater impact than the others to influence business success or failure? Should one category have greater influence than the others? Why or why not?

- What factors contributed to your team's effectiveness and successes? Consider things such as strategy, communication, training, planning, identification of best practices, and feedback.

- What factors were most challenging and difficult for your team to resolve? Consider how your team approached innovation, risk taking, problem solving, leadership, and diversity.

(30 minutes.)

Variations

- Occasionally during the activity interrupt the game to have all teams consider a "wild card" situation identified in advance of the activity. This situation may be one that you want the participants to consider relative to specific corporate strategies, initiatives, or challenges. The team that successfully answers the "wild card" situation can elect to move a block of their choice from either the bottom to the top of the tower or from the top back to the bottom of the tower.

- Solicit one team member from each group to take note of team strategies, dynamics, roles, discussions, ability to reach consensus, etc. The "observer" will report interesting observations out to the group at large at the conclusion of the activity.

<hr>

Submitted by Cheryl A. Brown.

Cheryl A. Brown, *president of Inspirational Learning Solutions Group, has more than twenty years of experience as a manager, human resources professional, and consultant. Ms. Brown was a featured speaker at the Association for Quality and Participation (AQP) Spring 2000 and ASTD TechKnowledge 2000 Conferences. She has a master's degree in human resources development and administration, is a certified manager (CM), and is a member of the Board of Regents of the Institute of Certified Professional Managers (ICPM).*

Towers Rule Sheet

Each tower represents your "company." As a manager of the company, your job is to work with the other members of your team to manage the affairs of the business in such a way as to ensure its viability and stability (in this case, to prevent the tower from falling down).

Process

The members of the team take turns doing the following:

1. Throw the colored cube.

2. Select a card from the appropriate stack as determined by the throw.

3. Read the card and briefly respond to or lead a discussion regarding the issue noted on the card.

4. Set the used card aside.

5. From the bottom half of the tower, identify a block that has the same color as the discarded card and cube.

6. Using one hand, remove the block from its current place in the tower and place it on top of the tower.

7. Continue until time has been called or until the tower falls.

Remember: The objective of the game is to properly manage the affairs of the business (answer the questions on the cards and transition the blocks) in such a way as to ensure the viability and stability of the business (prevent the tower from falling down).

Good luck and have fun.

Towers Customer Impact Cards

Name one issue relating to a Service Level Agreement (SLA) or other customer contract that is a concern for your operation.

Offer one suggestion on how to manage the issue more effectively.

You receive a Request for Proposal (RFP) from a possible new customer. The deadline to receive your response is ten business days from now.

What is the first step you will take to ensure that you meet the deadline?

A large sale to a global conglomerate will result in a significant amount of additional work, without additional resources.

How will you handle the additional work? How will you explain this to your team?

Customers continue to complain that you are reactive and only do something about a problem when they call it to your attention.

What can you do to change this perception and have them believe that you are proactive?

For three years in a row, your annual customer satisfaction survey has trended upward. The most recent survey showed a surprising decline in key areas.

How will you clarify the data?

You are moving from being a tech support team to a security response organization.

How will this decision impact your team?

The primary customer contact that you work with regularly left the company on short notice. You must now help to educate his replacement, who has no prior experience on your project.

Where do you begin?

You have become friendly with the customer advocate at a customer site. She is in a new position and does not have the necessary skills. You both know that the success of the upgrade to the latest products is critical to her success.

What do you do?

A rash of new viruses has resulted in a large number opf service delays and has impacted your workload and response times.

How will you explain this change in performance to your customers?

A former employee is now your primary contact for a major customer, who wants to know what you are doing to address new products, since the current market research is not identifying them.

How do you deal with this situation?

The 2006 Pfeiffer Annual: Consulting

Towers Employee Impact Cards

The cost of providing health care benefits is increasing to record heights. Employees are being required to increase their plan contributions.

What is the impact of this change on daily operations?

Employee satisfaction survey results have trended upward three years in a row. The last survey showed a surprising decline in a few key areas.

What suggestion do you have to better clarify the results?

Funding and time granted for employee training and development have historically increased year over year. For the first time, both must now be reduced.

How will you explain this to your team?

Samuel has been in the organization longer than anyone else. He is the best performer. He confided in you that he is planning to leave because he is bored and someone else offered him more money.

What do you do with this information?

To gain organizational efficiency, there will be a consolidation of some jobs. The result will be fewer promotions and more lateral job skills training.

How will this impact career development and morale?

To attract and retain the most qualified employees for the company, high salaries will be paid to new employees.

Do you think that high salaries alone guarantee high performance?

Consider the difference between traditional styles of management (command and control) and contemporary styles of leadership (coaching).

Which style do you think is more effective in your organization and why?

Many corporations consider that the cultural and ethnic diversity of their workforce is a strategic asset.

Describe the benefits that your corporation receives from having a diverse workforce.

Organizational policies and practices are important to organizations. They answer "who," "what," "where," "when," "why," and "how."

Name one policy or practice that you would like to see changed.

Your team is the best performing team in the organization. As a reward, you are moved to a low-performing team to "get them on track."

What impact will this move have on your high-performing team?

Introduction
to the Editor's Choice Section

Unfortunately, in the past we have had to reject exceptional ideas that did not meet the criteria of one of the sections or did not fit into one of our categories. So we recently created an Editor's Choice section that allows us to publish unique items that are useful to the profession rather than turn them down. This collection of contributions simply does not fit in one of the other three sections: Experiential Learning Activities; Inventories, Questionnaires, and Surveys; or Articles and Discussion Resources.

Based on the reason for creating this section, it is difficult to predict what you may find. You may anticipate a potpourri of topics, a variety of formats, and an assortment of categories. Some may be directly related to the training and consulting fields, and others may be related tangentially. Some may be obvious additions, and others may not. What you are sure to find is something you may not have expected but that will contribute to your growth and stretch your thinking. Suffice it to say that this section will provide you with a variety of useful ideas, practical strategies, and creative ways to look at the world. The material will add innovation to your training and consulting knowledge and skills. The contributions will challenge you to think differently, consider a new perspective, and add information you may not have considered before. The section will stretch your view of training and consulting topics.

The 2006 Pfeiffer Annual: Consulting includes two editor's choice items. One is an activity and one is an article. Both have valuable information for the consulting professional, but do not fit in the topic categories. Keep in mind the purpose for this section—good ideas that don't fit in the other sections.

Activity

> The Stigma of Stereotypes: Lessons for Youth in Being Different,
> by Kathryn Carson Key Whitehead

Article

> Communities of Competence as Catalysts for Change, by Elizabeth A. Smith

The Stigma of Stereotypes
Lessons for Youth in Being Different

Activity Summary

This activity is written for teenagers to help them learn about stereotyping.

Goals

- To help teens understand the harmful effects of stereotyping.

- To experience what it is like to be different, included, or excluded.

- To encourage youth to appreciate their similarities and differences.

Group Size

16 to 72 (multiples of 8) participants—as many as the room will allow—standing and moving around.

Time Required

30 minutes.

Materials

Note cards, prepared in advance—one for each participant.

Physical Setting

Tables and chairs for initial seating. A room large enough for circulation of all participants. Moving around is critical.

Facilitating Risk Rating

Moderate.

Preparation

1. Before meeting with the group, list eight "common" stereotypes or "labels" for the types of individual you are working with. When you know how many people you will have in the total group, separate index cards into sets, labeling eight of the cards in each set with one of the stereotypes each. For teens, the following stereotypes work well: Preppie, Drama Kid, Thug, Jock, Stoner (drug-user), Goth, Top 10 Academic, and Nerd.

2. Number the other side of each card, 1 through 8, reserving *one card* numbered 9, which you will substitute for a different card at some point. The numbers should be randomly assigned across stereotypes, except you will give the 9 to only one person in the total group. There should only be one card with the number 9 on it.

3. Next create a list of eight activities that can occur in anyone's life to make him or her feel separated or excluded (for example, for young people: 1 = teen pregnancy, 2 = victim of abuse, 3 = friend committed suicide, 4 = ran away from home, 5 = earned a bad reputation, 6 = failed out of high school/college, 7 = were convicted of a crime, 8 = have a drug or alcohol abuse problem). On the list to be associated with the number 9 card, give a more appreciated category, such as earning a full scholarship to an Ivy League college.

Process

1. As people come in, have everyone take a seat wherever they wish, because they will commonly sit with friends rather than people they do not know.

2. Shuffle the cards and go around and allow every individual to select one card. Hold them with the number side up so people will not select based on the stereotype.

3. Once everyone has received a card, tell him or her to flip it over to reveal what group (stereotype) they have just been assigned.

4. Tell everyone to form new groups based on their stereotypes. Assign spaces for each of the eight groups. Announce that they are now with their new group of friends, and they may associate *only with these people.* Give the groups a moment to settle in with each other. Allow everyone to shift into groups without

discussing the numbers on the other side of the cards. Ask them to think about what it feels like to be associated with that particular group.
(10 minutes.)

5. Speak to the group as a whole, asking them to refer to the numbers on the backs of their cards. Call out each number and announce the new predicament that goes with it based on your list. "If you have a number 1, you have just experienced _____."

6. Direct participants to come to the front of the room as you call out their numbers and predicaments. Be sure to pull people from the many different stereotype groups to the front of the room (make sure that the numbers do not correspond to the original groups). Go through the list down to number 8, calling them to the front of the room one at a time.
(10 minutes.)

7. When you are ready to read number 9, point out that there is only one person left in the audience. Ask: "Who is this individual going to share his or her accomplishment with?"

8. Conclude with these questions.

   • How did you feel about being in the first group of your own choosing?

   • How did you feel about having to change groups according to the stereotypes on your cards?

   • What does this tell you about stereotyping?

   • What did you learn about yourself as you heard the predicaments I listed to regroup you at the front of the room.

   • What will you do back at school as a result of what you learned from this exercise?
   (10 minutes.)

9. Sum up with: "Everyone stereotypes someone, whether it's the new kid at school or the new person in the office. But we rarely take the time to discover what common traits link people together. All people have shared similar experiences during their lifetimes, like having a friend pass away or winning a tough battle in life. If we all took a little more time to learn about our similarities, we wouldn't be sharing our accomplishments with just ourselves; we could share them with everyone."

Submitted by Kathryn Carson Key Whitehead.

Kathryn Carson Key Whitehead *is the 18-year-old daughter of M.K. Key, Ph.D., a frequent contributor to the Annuals. Whitehead has watched her mother teach since she was four. After she performed this exercise for her Critical Thinking class, she said, "Mom, I was you!"*

Communities of Competence as Catalysts for Change

Elizabeth A. Smith

Summary

The author's concept of Community of Competence™ is a framework and methodology to describe, assess, and combine separate strengths and core competencies of individuals, groups, and organizations into a meaningful whole. Each community of competence consists of a team of highly skilled and specialized people who have proven skills, abilities, and knowledge or competencies. Work assignments and roles performed are clearly defined to maximize job fit and streamline work efforts to increase productivity. These goal-oriented, flexible, dynamic groups resemble learning organizations and can readily respond to today's constantly changing work demands and environments.

In this article, the roles competence and socialization play in the evolution and maintenance of these highly cohesive groups are discussed. The importance of communication, knowledge, knowledge management, emotional intelligence, and leadership are examined. Reasons to create communities and detailed steps outlining ways to form and maintain these communities are provided.

Evolution of Communities of Competence

Competence as a Driving Force

The drive to reach and maintain self-imposed levels of competence, or job-related standards of excellence, is a longstanding intrinsic motivator that produces self-fulfillment (White, 1959). Competence includes skills, abilities, knowledge, experience, and other talents individuals and groups acquire over time. Individual and group competencies are prime driving forces in the formation and life of communities of competence. Most people know their strengths and limitations and can describe them. They also know when they are working at or above the expected level or self-imposed level. It is personally and professionally rewarding when individuals have the opportunity to apply learning in ways that enable them to gradually move to higher levels of competence.

Demonstrated and self-perceived competence or efficacy affect how people think and act, how they value each other, and how others value them. Competencies range from bits of information people store in their heads, such as a phone number, to specific competencies documented in precise form in printed and electronic formats, such as operators' manuals. Level of self-assessed competence is directly related to actual level of performance. If you think you are competent in an area, you probably are.

Competence is a highly desired quality in today's increasingly competitive, technologically oriented, fast-paced, networked world, where workers must often "do more with less" and "hit the ground running." Organizations must also remain competitive and innovative by reducing their costs and expanding their markets. The competencies and talents of people, the organization's most valuable resource, are seldom considered when partnerships or strategic alliances are formed to increase market share and profits.

A competency is created by forming various separate joint relationships between people, technology, organizational culture, organizational structure, and the environment. Hundreds of thousands of different types and levels of competencies are needed to meet the current, often cyclic workplace demands. For instance, "exploration competencies," or the ability to harvest ideas and expertise from many sources and apply know-how from outside parties and other businesses, are in high demand (Wolpert, 2002).

Most types and levels of competencies are shared through the socialization processes that occur when people actively work together and exchange information and knowledge. Personal socialization follows the same three sequential stages as organizational socialization: (1) learning about the new group, (2) first encounter with the new group, and (3) making full entry into the group by working together and sharing tacit knowledge or "know how" based on experience and common sense and on mentoring and learning from others (Greenberg & Baron, 2002).

Socialization and Self-Actualization

Socialization is the process of social interaction, enabling people to learn about standards and norms for acceptable behavior. It is about being with others. People who work together to solve problems satisfy their need for belongingness by sharing work experiences and knowledge. Socialization, a positive, highly desired motivator, is the second-highest level need in Maslow's (1943) five-level need hierarchy.

Group members who work in their areas of competence and are appropriately recognized and rewarded for their achievements meet their need for self-fulfillment or self-actualization, the highest level in Maslow's need hierarchy. The process of building human relationships and offering opportunities for socialization and self-fulfillment strengthen bonds between people and their unique and complementary competencies.

Managers who set goals too high or too low fail to realize that their employees are not motivated. Motivation is reportedly the highest when chances for success are 50/50 (Hampton, Summer, & Webber, 1978). Few managers know how to effectively use a person's self-assessed and demonstrated competence when making work assignments and doing performance evaluations.

Organizations are now (re)discovering the value of socialization or experience gained in face-to-face discussions, mentoring, apprenticeships, and accidental meetings at informal locations, such as the company cafeteria. The processes of observation, imitation, and other forms of personal contact provide opportunities to experience a sense of belonging, togetherness, and community.

A strong sense of community tends to correlate positively with exceptional company performance (Mauro, 2002). Socialization processes that occur outside one's community also enable each community member to share interests, concerns, specialized information, and unique knowledge with peers and work associates.

Communities

Observed and recorded competencies of people have always provided a basis for forming boundaryless communities. For hundreds of thousands of years, people around the world used their competencies to survive famines, invasions, and other catastrophic events. Need for food and safety were major cyclic forces contributing to the creation of these protective communities. Community members used their talents, experience, and material resources to meet specific needs and cope with their unpredictable environments.

The evolution of communities has been a long, slow process. Communities are gradually becoming more specialized in order to improve the use of their human and material resources. Intact communities, unlike traditional groups, give members personal and professional support. They provide members with a personal identity and recognize members' accomplishments. From the organizational standpoint, community can be a physical location where people go to exchange ideas, share knowledge, and experience a sense of professional identity or status. Many organizations define community in terms of shared values and common goals. Community is becoming the new metaphor for organizations.

Historically, man's survival depended on his ability to live and work in supportive social networks. The same is true today. Sociology, social psychology, group dynamics, politics, management, and other disciplines have influenced the formation, use, and activities common to both social networks and communities. Two types of communities contributing to the formation of communities of competence are described below.

Communities of Interest

These communities are like social clubs or philanthropic groups and share interests and concerns. Members derive benefit from interpersonal relationships and celebrate achievements, such as successful fund-raising activities. For example, members of Xerox's business communities of interest work together on specific projects to build knowledge for their company and themselves through informal communication and contact (Smith, 2001a; Tobin, 1997).

Communities of Practice

Communities of practice date back to ancient times (Wenger & Snyder, 2000). In classical Greece, communities of practice existed as "corporations," or groups of masons, artisans, and other craftsmen. These self-selected, informal groups within and outside traditional organizations are bound together by their shared expertise and dedication to a common mission or desire to solve specific problems. People who join communities of practice know they have something to give to the community and are eager to participate. Professional societies, as communities of practice, unite members from various disciplines and numerous organizations so that they can share current competencies and acquire new competencies.

Communities of practice renew themselves by generating, acquiring, and processing new information and knowledge. To illustrate, over one hundred worldwide communities of practice at the World Bank are linked together to continually expand and improve the quality of their knowledge base (Pascarella, 1997).

Knowledge is the engine that powers current communities of practice. If a company is to make the best use of the knowledge it has, it must know what local knowledge exists and also its relative value. It must "know what it knows" (Brown & Dugid, 2000).

Communities of Competence

The author's concept of Community of Competence™ is a further extension of communities of practice and communities of interest. A Community of Competence is "a framework and methodology to describe, assess, and combine separate strengths and core competencies of individuals, groups, and organizations into a meaningful whole" (Smith, 2005, p. 8).

Table 1 presents major ways communities and regular work groups differ. There is no clear division between these two types of groups nor any pure "regular" groups or pure communities of competence. Boundaries are permeable, and some descriptions overlap.

Table 1.   Comparison of Regular Work Groups and Communities of Competence

Who	Regular Work Groups	Community of Competence
Membership	Members of groups assigned to do a specific job.	Primary focus of members is on solving problems or achieving common goals.
Membership Selection	Work for organization; hired to perform specific job.	Selected based on known current competence or potential to demonstrate competence.
Type of Group	Set by organization or intact work group. Could be a team, cross-functional group, or high-performance team.	Flexible, but highly structured, depending on need. Membership rotates due to work assignments.
Size of Group	Two to 100 people, depending on task.	Two to thousands of people in standard/virtual groups.
How		
Methods and Tools	Traditional work methods, networking face-to-face, electronic, multimedia using existing tools and established work methods.	Synergies created from learning, sharing, and redesign/reinvention due to free flow of information, as in self-organizing systems. Often reinventing, redesigning existing methods, or creating state-of-the-art tools to fit existing needs. Use iterative methods, self-learning systems, and others to improve individual and group accomplishments.
Duration	Specific roles in serial projects, as needed by the organization.	Only when special talents are needed and may cycle in and out, as needed.
Leadership	The person assigned to lead the group.	Anyone who has the competence at a time when specific levels of competence or expertise are needed.
Accountability	To group/organizational leaders.	To coordinator outside the community.
Values	Conform to organizational culture.	Demonstrate strong values that are consistent with work project, not necessarily with those of the organization where members work.
When		
Work Period	During standard working hours.	Any time—24 hours/seven days a week.

(table continued on the next page)

Table 1. *continued*

Why	Regular Work Groups	Community of Competence
Purpose	As required by the organization to stay in business.	Develop state-of-the art solutions that grow and continue to evolve in unexpected ways.
Focus	Solve assigned problems using available resources.	Intense effort to identify and bring all needed resources from numerous sources to create innovative products and processes.
Sharing of Information	As required by organization's structure and rules for communication. Rarely volunteer information.	Use all channels and networks to exchange explicit and tacit knowledge on a continuous, spontaneous basis.
Power	Used as needed to meet goals.	Coordination and sharing drive all efforts.
Communication	As designed by organization's verbal standard and electronic communication networks.	Anywhere, all channels and all types of verbal, print, and electronic networks.
Driving Force	Profit motive or to meet goals in a specific period of time.	Mental and physical energy of members serves as intellectual catalyst to meet goals.
Stability	Ranges from low to high, depending on economics, task, and leadership.	High and intense while working on project.
Where		
Location	Inside the organization or connected to joint ventures, partners, etc.	Inside the organization, but may be connected electronically anywhere in the world, 24 hours a day, 7 days a week.
What		
Goals and Strategies	Complete the current project or as assigned.	Use all expertise for needed time period to achieve goal(s) for which group was formed.
Goals	As assigned or to meet group and organizational goals.	Achieve specific goal for which group was formed.

The common groupings of "who," "how," "when," "why," "where," and "what" summarize major concepts. Specific criteria are used to describe and illustrate work processes and methods, the dynamics of groups, and type of work assignments.

Work processes shown in Table 1 provide practical selection criteria and guidelines to set up communities. "Best" work processes outlined in Table 1 can be used to compare the two groups and select characteristics that are known to increase group productivity. Descriptions of community of competence activities can be used to design "ideal" groups to solve specific problems quickly.

This new group form is proposed as a variation to standard cross-disciplinary, cross-functional, high performance, and autonomous teams or work groups. Communities of competence are highly specialized, focused, cohesive groups. They are more able to meet the needs of increasingly demanding customers and adjust to the current economically driven, highly competitive work environment than conventional groups are. Overall, this new form of group has the potential to provide a template to create, motivate, streamline, and maximize the productivity of groups and improve the quality of resulting work processes, services, and products (Smith, 2005). Work groups that function as intact, focused, cohesive communities have more opportunity and greater potential to maximize how human and material resources are used than any other currently existing type of work group.

The community of competence framework provides a supportive infrastructure, communication networks, and a central operating core to handle the basic business processes of organizing, planning, staffing, directing, and monitoring results. The formation, size, and life span of communities are shaped and guided by professional relationships, informal and formal communication networks, and workplace demands.

Shared values, strong organizational culture, and socialization help create, define, build, and maintain communities of competence. To illustrate, a community made up of engineers, marketing people, and sales people jointly design and market new products. The combined expertise of each member and their focus on design and functionality can foster cooperation, decrease wasted efforts, time, and cost, and reduce time to complete the project.

Communities of competence consist of individuals who have special or unique talents, expertise, and core competencies needed to achieve specific work goals. Membership size ranges from a few members assigned to solve one specific problem to members of many organizations working on a huge project, such as building the world's tallest skyscraper.

These flexible, dynamic communities are knowledge-based organizations or mini-learning organizations in which continual learning is encouraged, supported, and rewarded. People in learning organizations acquire their knowledge, abilities, and skills from a variety of sources within and beyond their organizations. They openly share their talents with others, strive to achieve professional and company goals, and are empowered to try new ideas and work methods to improve their own and the company's performance (Smith, 1995; Tobin, 1997).

Communities of competence resemble living systems. They use face-to-face contacts and electronic or wireless networks from anywhere in the world to link people, processes, data, and information to exchange knowledge and accomplish specific tasks. For example, people from the smallest, most geographically remote communities can solve their problems locally by electronically linking up with the resources of vast multinational organizations currently described as "global brains." Global insights are combined with competencies of local managers (Dutton, 1999). Virtual and electronic communities of competence are easy to build, but often difficult to maintain. Working alone is not ideal because personal contact, a key element in socialization, is eliminated.

The unique personalities and characteristics of people—their interrelationships, communication, and knowledge—form the heart of the community. They can grow spontaneously or emerge due to a work-related need or be learner and/or customer driven. Communities of competence cannot be built or maintained unless there are strong interpersonal relationships and actual or virtual two-way communication networks joining separate communities.

Communities of competence, unlike communities of practice and communities of interest, are based on demonstrated competencies needed to reach goals or solve problems. After the problem is solved or the project completed, members of these communities either move to a new community where their unique talents are again in demand or are sought out by those requiring their unique abilities and knowledge.

Communities of competence are predicted to exist at all five stair-stepped levels of competence: novice, advanced beginner, proficient, expert, and world class (Drejer, 2001). Drejer believes that keeping pace with constantly changing technologies means that new competencies must be acquired every three to five years. This provides a strong case for ongoing training and development, on-the-job training, mentoring, and certification. What is measured and documented gets done. Therefore, peers (who are hard to fool), team leaders, and supervisors should all assess competence and submit separate performance evaluations.

There are no pure work groups and no pure communities of competence. Due to variations in personality, interests, values, abilities, knowledge, experience, and work assignments, community members differ widely. Communities remain intact when members are committed to and interested in a specific work activity and maintain their level of performance. When members focus on subtle differences in their agendas, factors that first united members rarely keep them together. Some members will rotate between communities of practice and communities of competence until their needs for competence, socialization, and recognition are met.

While there may be great variety within communities of competence, a few pivotal factors affect their formation: communication, knowledge and knowledge management, and leadership and emotional intelligence.

Communication

Communication underlies all human activities. It plays a prime role in communities of competence by linking members together through informal networks involving direct contact, such as conversations, mentoring, observing, teaching, and brainstorming, all of which involve exchanging tacit knowledge. Some communication is planned, but many exchanges develop spontaneously or result from people's proximity to one another.

Much data, information, and knowledge is co-created and openly shared in informal networks. Unfortunately, some organizations treat informal networks as an invisible enemy that inhibits decision making and keeps work from happening (Cross & Prusak, 2002). These intricate, informal communication webs are often considered unobservable and ungovernable. There may be so many informal networks that senior managers either work around them or ignore these potentially rich sources of information and tacit knowledge. When links between people, particularly in large and globally distributed corporations, are underused or misunderstood, much key tacit information or knowledge people carry in their heads is lost. Information not yet formalized by memos, reports, or proposals is also lost.

Roles

People play four major types of roles in informal communication networks: central connectors, boundary spanners, information brokers, and peripheral specialists (Cross & Prusak, 2002).

Central connectors link together people in informal networks. They know who has expertise or key information. Central connectors are easily recognized, as they talk the most, answer questions, and provide background information.

Boundary spanners communicate information to central connectors and consult with and advise people by nurturing connections between people of differing types and levels of expertise who work outside the informal network or in other organizations. Few people can function as boundary spanners. Most people lack the breadth and depth of intellectual expertise and the wealth of social contacts and the personality traits they need to be accepted by vastly different groups.

Information brokers bind different subgroups or subnets of informal networks together by communicating across subgroups. Brokers help maintain a high level of effectiveness and keep splinter groups from forming. They wield the power of central connectors, but have fewer direct links than connectors.

Peripheral specialists are sought out by those needing specialized expertise, information, or technical knowledge. These "loners" usually stay on the edge of the informal network rather than associate too closely with people who work hard to stay on the cutting edge.

Knowledge and Knowledge Management

Information is data that has been given structure. *Knowledge is information that is combined with experience, context, interpretation, and reflection* (Smith, 1995). "A learning organization is an organization skilled at creating, acquiring, transferring knowledge, and at modifying its behavior to reflect new knowledge and insights" (Garvin, 1993, p. 80).

Members of communities of competence often use tacit knowledge to solve problems and share experiences and ideas. The amount of undocumented tacit knowledge grows daily and represents an individual's cumulative experiences achieved over a lifetime. Since most tacit knowledge is difficult to document, people carry it around in their heads. They use tacit knowledge to solve problems they have not encountered before and to come up with new ideas. No knowledge management (KM) system to adequately identify, document, store, and retrieve tacit knowledge currently exists.

Knowledge distribution from communities of competence resembles methods used in KM. For example, Monsanto uses the following steps in its KM process to do the following: (1) connect people with other knowledgeable people; (2) connect people with information; (3) enable the conversion of information to knowledge; (4) encapsulate knowledge to make it easier to transfer; and (5) disseminate knowledge around the firm (Junnarker, 1999).

Unless databases, formats, software, and hardware are designed to simplify efforts to retrieve and share results, each of the methods above will have limited success. Speed and adequacy of distribution systems remain major problem areas in knowledge management, as few KM systems address the entire knowledge process. Still fewer adequately codify and send documented knowledge to people when it is wanted and in a format that is easy to understand. These competence-based communities are excellent sources of highly selective, practical information and knowledge that can be used to make KM systems more effective and user-friendly.

Emotional Intelligence and Leadership

Emotional intelligence or emotional quotient (EQ) is the ability to manage ourselves and our relationships effectively. In the last ten years, EQ has gradually been accepted as a prime factor in leadership (Goleman, 2004).

The four major factors of EQ include self-awareness, self-management, social awareness, and social skills. *Self-awareness* relates to understanding one's competencies, the core of communities of competence. *Self-management* focuses on achievement, initiative, motivation, and adaptability. *Social awareness* includes ability to build decision-making networks, read current level of organizational life, and recognize and meet customers' needs. *Social skills* include teamwork and the ability to build bonds, develop others, and inspire others. The social skills of EQ and the communication skills used to manage relationships and socialization in communities of competence are similar.

Advantages of a Community of Competence

This section gives practical guidelines on the following benefits of forming a community of competence and how to encourage each one: (1) sharing knowledge, (2) enhancing performance and productivity, (3) motivation, (4) using creativity to increase profit, (5) adding value for customers, (6) creating and maintaining a trained workforce, (7) improving current knowledge management systems, and (8) stimulating change.

From the view of productivity, both high performance teams and communities of competence are designed to achieve their goals and objectives as quickly and efficiently as possible. However, unlike high performance teams, community team members are pre-screened and evaluated so proof exists that they have the required type and level of competencies and a history of success. For example, a software developer in a community of competence must have the necessary professional credentials, a proven track record, and demonstrate expertise in his or her own area and also experience in working with marketing and sales people.

Ideally, communities of competence guide and chart the flow of communication, thought, and action by building bridges between people and their islands of knowledge. Competencies are dynamic, constantly changing and evolving. Value increases when competencies are shared, applied, refined, improved, and passed on to others who then recycle and reuse them or create new competencies. This upward, endless, self-perpetuating spiral of competence raises levels of thought and action and is an excellent intrinsic or non-monetary motivator.

Sharing Knowledge

Sharing knowledge is vital to the existence and success of members and enhances their abilities to solve problems, be creative, and maintain competence (Smith, 2001b).

Arrange for a real or virtual space for members to meet together and think, be creative, and steadily and systematically expand their knowledge. Telecommuting and electronic networking rarely provide ways to meet and exchange ideas and fulfil social and belongingness needs.

Use intrinsic or non-monetary motivators to appropriately reward and recognize people for sharing tacit and explicit knowledge through information networks. Outcomes would be the reduced overall costs to do business. Similarly, efficiency of KM processes would increase when knowledge flows directly to those needing it.

Enhancing Individual Performance and Productivity

Use synergy, streamline work processes, and leverage competencies to maximize job fit.

Create synergy by fostering and supporting a mindset to encourage cross-disciplinary, cross-functional communication to raise levels of professional and organizational competence. Encourage members to contribute what they know and recognize and appropriately reward them for their efforts to improve performance.

Improve job fit by identifying work process and the level of competence of members needed to reach the assigned goals. Mobilize resources where multiple competencies are needed (Smith, 2005). Leveraging and combining competencies can reduce the size of the gap between what managers want and what members are able to do and actually do.

Raise levels of professional and organizational competence through authentic conversations that occur in open communication channels and informal gatherings. Many conversations will convey tacit knowledge, an ingredient vital to gaining and maintaining a competitive edge.

Fine-tune key work processes, such as decision making and problem solving, to help members to come up to speed quickly. These "super groups" are skilled at knowing how to capture, use, and disseminate the steadily growing untapped, often undocumented, reservoir of explicit and tacit knowledge in the group. Members' ability to acquire, understand, and apply knowledge effectively (do the right thing) and efficiently (do things right) enables them to be more productive by streamlining and maximizing their efforts.

Enable members to spend more time in their areas of competence to experience fulfillment through peer recognition. Competent competence development is a first step in the move from professional to world class (Drejer, 2001).

Motivation

Beliefs and attitudes reflecting "motivated self-interest" or "what's in it for me?" reduce motivation. Managers who are predictable and consistent in their use of intrinsic motivators, such as flexible working hours or gift certificates for a job well done, can gradually raise employees' levels of motivation.

Encourage members to share job-related competencies and knowledge and to communicate openly with each other when they work toward a common goal. Work groups that function as intact, focused, motivated communities have an excellent opportunity and potential to streamline and improve the ways human and material resources are used. For example, when members discuss and evaluate their own talent and areas of competence, they gain insights into the best way to use their abilities and do their jobs. They also know what talents, tools, technologies, and other resources are required to enable them to work at the upper end of their capacities by achieving self-actualization.

Increase the sharing and flow of tacit and explicit or academic knowledge within and between communities of competence by building intrinsic incentives into work processes and the performance evaluation process. Numeric and descriptive peer evaluations of cooperation and sharing, for instance, can be embedded into performance appraisals. Peers can design the evaluations and assess their own group members.

Using Creativity to Increase Profit

Creativity and innovation are often considered competitive marketplace weapons. Visionary leaders who recognize and endorse creative efforts will help their organizations retain their competitive edge. Unfortunately, few organizations provide a culture that supports and rewards creativity and innovation.

Creativity thrives in supportive organizational cultures. Sharing undocumented, state-of-the-art tacit knowledge enables members to take risks and design innovative products and services. These organizations gradually move ahead of their competition.

Creativity wanes during mergers, acquisitions, partnering, and building alliances to temporarily reduce cost. Employees eventually do more work in less time. As job stress increases, creativity, job satisfaction, and group and company loyalty decrease. Worse yet, the drive to reduce costs and produce cheaper services and products may lower quality and create dissatisfied customers.

Adding Value for Customers

Value is often considered to be "what the customer says it is" or is based on customers' expectations or perceptions.

Identify and use the rich resources of community members and their high-level, unique work output to go one step beyond the level of value customers ask for.

Value is added when customers' expectations, perceptions, and what they really want are known. Value is also added by the synergy produced by searching out, documenting, and deliberately combining and sharing the single "best of the best" work processes, products, or services created by individuals, groups, or organizations.

Creating and Maintaining a Trained Workforce

One of the biggest business-related problems is hiring, training, and maintaining a capable workforce. People must be encouraged to continually expand their knowledge base and expertise through classroom and non-traditional training, perhaps through e-learning. Upgrading one's core competencies to remain employable and acquiring new competencies must become a way of life.

Members of communities have proven core competencies that are in great demand. A prime asset is their store of tacit knowledge.

Help members to continually meet job requirements and expand their portfolio of talents by using content area experts, leaders in their respective fields, and input from management. Since members know their competencies, they will be able to document existing competencies and expand their overall portfolio of competencies (Smith, 1999).

Apply current technologies to support continual learning. Satellite communications, web-based networks, asynchronous electronic connections, such as chat rooms, news groups, conferencing systems, and joint document preparation, among others, will change the direction and focus of educational systems and institutions of higher learning (Farson & Keyes, 2002).

Improving Current Knowledge Management Systems

Users or customers of KM systems are more likely to cause changes in the status quo and improvements through "grass roots" efforts than by following management's edict.

The underlying theory, operating framework, and guiding principles of communities of competence can be applied to streamline current KM systems by introducing standard taxonomies, improving operational definitions, and applying systems thinking.

Much tacit knowledge is generated in socialization processes, such as sharing work experiences and brainstorming. Gathering, classifying, documenting, and retrieving this valuable tacit knowledge will be extremely beneficial now and in the future.

Stimulating Change

The gradual development and effective use of communities of competence is an evolutionary change process that occurs one small step at a time.

Involve designated or self-selected champions in creating and supporting streamlined, focused work groups, such as communities of competence. Use print and electronic media to "showcase" or promote exemplary communities. Provide support systems and a methodology to encourage and reward positive behavioral and structural organizational changes. It is vital to have strategically placed champions and strong, inspired, visionary leaders. Making everyone a champion is a good way to foster change and improvement and to ensure success of change efforts. Each champion can be responsible for some facet of change.

Use communities of competence as work-process-based catalysts for change. The array of experiences members have and their numerous multidisciplinary and cross-functional contacts will help break down barriers that previously prevented the open sharing of knowledge and expertise (Smith, 2005).

Members of these collaborative work groups can encourage one another and those outside their groups to redirect their thought processes and behaviors to include thinking, acting, behaving, and evaluating in terms of specific, clearly defined levels of documented competencies.

Shared values and a strong, intact organizational culture are prime factors in building and maintaining a community of competence. Creating a strong supportive organizational culture that rewards and recognizes superior performance is a major first step. To achieve success, involve top management.

Steps to Creating a Community of Competence

The following section presents an overall framework and guidelines for creating a community of competence.

1. *Use systems thinking to view the entire work process and then determine how each step fits into the overall goals.* This systems or "holistic" view first introduced by Likert (1967) enables us to see a unit as a whole first and then see how separate parts fit together and how each relates to the other. Feedback loops used for control and correction connect each part of the system with every other part of the system. Systems thinking can be used to select members, match their competencies to the job, and identify work processes, procedures, and goals to be accomplished, along with the timelines.

2. *Create and use precise, clearly defined concepts and methodologies to maximize "job fit" or match people with the tasks and jobs to be done.* Define competencies in operational terms that state the exact work processes, what is to be done, what is expected, and how the concept will be used (Drejer, 2001; Smith, 1997). Hands-on users and their team leaders—not supervisors or management—must develop operational definitions of concepts. Each person using these concepts must define them, agree on what each means, and then use them. For instance, engineers define productivity as "useful work/energy = 1" and accountants as "profit/sales."

3. *Develop a simple, user-friendly taxonomy.* Taxonomy is the science or technique of classification originally used to identify, name, and group organisms. Currently, taxonomies use operational definitions to define the entire scope of a task or event, from the first to the last step. Methods used to create the taxonomy and the results parallel the

organization's methods to manage knowledge. Leibowitz and Beckman's (1998) eight-step approach—identify, capture, select, store, share, apply, create, and sell—can be applied to managing knowledge in each community of competence. Health care leaders from academic institutions, government agencies, and health care institutions are developing a taxonomy of medical terms, practices, and procedures. This taxonomy is being evaluated for use worldwide to help standardize and improve diagnosis and treatment of patients. Most taxonomies remain a work in progress as new terms are defined and classified and other terms are updated.

4. *Draw communication networks and planning and thinking process maps to identify the positions, relationships, and competencies of key people.* Maps that are kept current provide invaluable information for current and future use.

5. *Build flexibility into work processes and activities to allow for change without sacrificing people, ideas, or ownership.* Use systems thinking and "reverse scenario building" to create an image or scenario of the type of work to be done and the level and types of skills, abilities, and knowledge needed. Start with the completed scenario and work backward, one step at a time, until you reach the first step. Write down each step. Then review each step to be certain the entire work process has been adequately described and documented. Use various steps of this process to design separate units or modules of core or shared activities that are easy to interchange or adapt.

6. *Determine different levels of competencies for various types of work and how often these competencies are needed and actually used.* Create a registry or a complete printed or electronic file of pertinent information from individuals and groups. Record the type of problems, solutions, and names of community members. Use lessons learned to solve similar problems or select new community members based on their expertise.

7. *Encourage and reward continual learning (Senge, 1990), double-loop learning, or learning about what we are learning (Argyris, 1994; Argyris & Schon, 1978).* Continual learning, the heart of all knowledge-based systems, plays a key role in communities of competence.

Example of a Functioning Community of Competence

Hospitals, clinics, health maintenance organizations, ambulatory care centers, nursing homes, and other health care providers, such as physicians, nurses, and therapists, need to share knowledge and experience. The common focus should be on identifying and using competencies to work together to improve the quality of patient care and increase patient safety and satisfaction. Champions in health care are now leading massive efforts and share and disseminate knowledge.

Information technology, such as tele-medicine, has the potential to reach people regardless of location. Communication systems that are both paper-based and electronically based record the patient's status and provide vital feedback to monitor progress. In-service programs, grand rounds, continuing education courses, one-on-one discussions, and mentoring are rich sources of explicit and tacit knowledge that can be directly applied in patient care settings.

Dotan (2002) first applied the author's concept of communities of competence to health care. Communities of competence gradually evolved into a whole when separate health care groups combined efforts to achieve common goals. Members provide a range of solutions for specific heath-related needs (Dotan, 2002). For instance, physicians who have patients with multiple problems require multiple services—radiology, surgery, physical therapy, and the pharmacy, each with its own community of competence. Coordination and communication between communities are vital to the quality of patient care and patient satisfaction. Today, few separate departments readily share medical records due to different forms and databases used in medical records, incompatible software, and some personal or professional reluctance to share. Thinking together is a major first step in bringing people together.

Summary and Conclusions

The author's concept of community of competence provides a framework and support system that enables members to work in their areas of competence and be adequately recognized and rewarded for their performance, thus increasing their productivity. There are numerous professional benefits of mobilizing the competencies of people and applying current knowledge to help solve the growing number of marketplace demands.

To survive in today's highly competitive, global marketplace, organizations' leaders should determine competencies of their employees and place them in jobs that allow full use of their overall talents.

The steps to build and maintain a community of competence can be used to create a new form of group that can focus on specific ways to improve both overall work quality and productivity. Positive synergy generated by focusing on helping people do what they do best lets them deal more effectively with mounting economic pressures to "work harder and faster." Building vision, mission, goals, and strategies around core competencies increases everyone's chances for success.

References

Agryris, C. (1994). Good communication that blocks learning. *Harvard Business Review,* 72(4), 77–85.

Argyris, C., & Schon, D.A. (1978). *Organizational learning: A theory of action perspective.* Reading, MA: Addison-Wesley.

Brown, J.S., & Dugid, P. (2000). Balancing act: How to capture knowledge without killing it. *Harvard Business Review, 78*(3), 73–80.

Cross, R., & Prusak, L. (2002). The people who make organizations go—or stop. *Harvard Business Review, 80*(6), 104–112.

Dotan, D.B. (2002, Spring). Communities of competence: A concept behind implementation of quality improvement and patient safety centers in health care. *American Society for Quality,* Health Care Division Spring Newsletter, pp. 10–11.

Drejer, A. (2001). A case of competence development. *International Journal of Business Performance Management, 3*(1), 90–106.

Dutton, G. (1999, May). Building a global brain. *Management Review,* pp. 34–38.

Farson, R., & Keyes, R. (2002). The failure-tolerant leader. *Harvard Business Review, 80*(8), 64–71.

Garvin, D. (1993, July/August). Building a learning organization, *Harvard Business Review,* pp. 78–91.

Goleman, D. (2004). What makes a leader? *Harvard Business Review, 82*(1), 82, 84–91.

Greenberg, J., & Baron, R.A. (2002). *Behavior in organizations.* Upper Saddle River, NJ: Prentice Hall.

Hampton, D.R., Summer, C.R., & Webber, R.A. (1978*). Organizational behavior and the practice of management.* Glenview, IL: Scott, Foresman.

Junnarkar, B. (1999). Creating fertile ground for knowledge management at Monsanto. *Perspectives on Business Innovation* 1. Available: www.businessinnovation.ey.com/journal/issue1/features/creati/loader,html.

Leibowitz, J., & Beckman, T. (1998). *Knowledge organizations: What every manager should know.* Boca Raton, FL: St. Lucie/CRC Press.

Likert, R. (1967). *The human organization.* New York: McGraw-Hill.

Mauro, T. (2002). Helping organizations build community. *Training & Development, 1*(4), 52–58.

Maslow, A.H. (1943). A dynamic theory of human motivation. *Psychology Review, 50,* 370–396.

Pascarella, P. (1997, October). Harnessing knowledge. *Management Review,* pp. 37–40.

Senge, P. (1990). *The fifth discipline.* New York: Doubleday.

Smith, E.A. (1995, October/November). Productivity: The challenge of the learning organization. *The Quality Observe*r, pp. 16–18.

Smith, E.A. (1997). Operational definitions: An aid in benchmarking quality. In *The 1997 Annual: Volume 2, Consulting* (pp. 237–254). San Francisco, CA: Pfeiffer.

Smith, E.A. (1999). The core-unique-expanding model: The career passport for performance. *International Journal of Business Performance Management, 1*(3), 252–264.

Smith, E.A. (2001a). Achieving a balanced work life. *The 2001 Annual: Volume 2, Consulting* (pp. 145–154). San Francisco, CA: Pfeiffer.

Smith, E.A. (2001b). The role of tacit and explicit knowledge in the workplace. *Journal of Knowledge Management, 5*(4), 311–321.

Smith, E.A. (2005). Communities of competence: New resources in the workplace. *The Journal of Workplace Learning,* Special Edition, *17*(1/2), 7–23.

Tobin, D.R. (1997). *Intellectual capital.* New York: Doubleday/Currency.

Wenger, E.C., & Snyder, W.M. (2000). Communities of practice: The organizational frontier. *Harvard Business Review, 78*(1), 139–145.

White, R.W. (1959). Motivation reconsidered: The concept of competence. *Psychological Review,* 66, 297–334.

Wolpert, J.D. (2002). Breaking out of the innovation box. *Harvard Business Review, 80*(8), 76–83.

www.communityofcompetence.com describes and illustrates the steadily growing medical communities of competence that include separate professional disciplines and government and non-government organizations.

Community of Competence is officially trademarked as Community of Competence™.

Elizabeth A. Smith, *Ph.D., is executive director of CRG Medical Foundation for Patient Safety, a Houston, Texas-based non-profit foundation. She has taught numerous management courses at the University of Houston Clear Lake and Rice University. She has published over forty peer-reviewed articles. Dr. Smith's publications include* Creating Productive Organizations *(St. Lucie/CRC Press) and* The Productivity Manual *(Gulf Publishing/Butterworth-Heinemann). She belongs to Sigma Xi, American Society for Quality, American College of Health Care Executives, and the Gulf Coast Association for Healthcare Quality.*

Introduction

to the Inventories, Questionnaires, and Surveys Section

Inventories, questionnaires, and surveys are valuable tools for the HRD professional. These feedback tools help respondents take an objective look at themselves and at their organizations. These tools also help to explain how a particular theory applies to them or to their situations.

Inventories, questionnaires, and surveys are useful in a number of training and consulting situations: privately for self-diagnosis; one-on-one to plan individual development; in a small group to open discussion; in a work team to help the team to focus on its highest priorities; or in an organization to gather data to achieve progress. You will find that the use of inventories, questionnaires, and surveys enriches, personalizes, and deepens training, development, and intervention designs. Many can be combined with other experiential learning activities or articles in this or other *Annuals* to design an exciting, involving, practical, and well-rounded intervention. Each instrument includes the background necessary for understanding, presenting, and using it. Interpretive information, scales, and scoring sheets are also provided. In addition, we include the reliability and validity data contributed by the authors. If you wish additional information on any of these instruments, contact the authors directly. You will find their addresses and telephone numbers in the "Contributors" listing near the end of this volume.

The 2006 Pfeiffer Annual: Consulting includes two assessment tools in the following categories:

Leadership

Leadership Capability Assessment, by Teri B. Lund

Organizations

Motivational Climate Inventory, by K.S. Gupta

Leadership Capability Assessment

Teri B. Lund

Summary

This instrument was developed for use in assessing leadership development needs for both current leaders and those in succession planning programs. The results from the assessments can be used to take specific actions and list priorities in improving leadership skills and knowledge within your organization to gain the desired outcomes realized from strong leadership.

The purpose of this assessment is to evaluate current leadership and succession planning candidates for their developmental needs in three areas:

1. Core Skills (examples are decision making, managing change, problem solving, and communication).

2. Emotional Intelligence (examples are initiative, power, management capability, and logic ability).

3. Competitive Advantage Indicators (examples are institutionalization of the business strategy, cultural management, creativity, and innovation).

The instrument is administered much like a 360-degree evaluation, gaining input from peers, associates, and those who have reported to the individual.

Description of the Instrument

The Leadership Capability Assessment consist of a set of criteria used to identify developmental needs for leaders and potential leaders in the organization. Such criteria can, of course, be adapted by each organization to better correspond to specific needs that exist for that organization. The instrument is grouped in three key areas, with fifteen assessment items in each area. Each item is then followed by a traditional five-point Likert style rating scale ranging from 1 = Strongly Disagree to 5 = Strongly Agree. Additional space is provided at the end of the instrument for open-ended comments.

Analysis of the results can provide several views of the level of leadership skills within your organization. Examples of the types of information that can be gathered from the analysis include but are not limited to the following:

1. The developmental needs for the current leadership;

2. The developmental needs of the bench;

3. A development program for succession planning candidates; and/or

4. An overall leadership deficiency that is present within your organization that may be preventing it from reaching a higher level of competence, excellence, and competitiveness.

The items included in the Leadership Capability Assessment have been used in large and small organizations to assess current and future developmental needs for the leadership within those organizations and to identify bench developmental needs. The assessments have been met with strong acceptance and positive feedback. Assessment "owners" within the organizations have said that the instruments have given them tools that provide concrete and objective data as to what needs to be offered or changed within leadership training and succession planning. The corresponding leadership training that has been offered as a result of the inventories has provided strong outcomes for the organizations and the individual leaders and has increased the strength of benches within the organizational leadership.

Administration of the Assessment

Administration is not difficult. Simply follow the steps below:

1. Identify the participants for the assessment from the pools of current leaders, succession planning participants, or the bench itself. (The participants can be from all groups or from one distinct group. It is important to know which group they belong to for analysis purposes.)

2. Identify a method for coding the group the participants belong in. This can be as simple as putting a code on the assessment or color-coding of the assessments themselves.

3. Determine whether you will be doing a self-assessment only or using others' feedback. If you are doing a self-assessment only, skip to Step 6.

4. If you are including feedback from others, you will need to determine the process for identifying who will provide feedback for each assessment participant. For example, will you be using a combination of peer, associate, and staff feedback? It is important for analysis that those providing feedback are at consistent levels, assessment participant to assessment participant, for analysis and comparison purposes. (In other words do not use a peer for Participant A and staff for Participant B.) It is better to code the role of those providing feedback for consistency purposes.

5. Code the assessments for those providing feedback by feedback role (peer, associate, staff, manager) and code the assessments in relation to the participant the feedback is about.

6. Distribute the assessments to the participants chosen and to those chosen to provide feedback (if applicable), with an assigned due date.

7. Collate the data, analyze it, and prepare a report identifying the leadership skills present and lacking.

8. Set up a meeting with senior management to review the results and report back to the participants on leadership's strengths, developmental needs, and "next steps" the organization will take.

9. Develop an action plan for the leadership development program and begin working on that plan.

Scoring Process

The scoring for the Leadership Capability Assessment is somewhat dependent on whether or not your organization will be providing feedback from others as well as a self-report. If there is feedback from others, their scores will be reflected as an average for each item and overall category, such as Core Skills.

All responses are based on a 5–point scale and the scores are summed for each category.

Other Suggested Uses for the Instrument

Other organizations have used these instruments as part of a leadership development class. Participants completed their self-assessments as homework after the first class about leadership skills. Data from others was collated in advance and provided to the participants during the second day of class. During that class they compared their results with the feedback they received and completed the collation worksheet for themselves. They identified key learnings of the developmental areas they had for themselves and then reported out as a group, creating a chart and discussing potential "leadership weaknesses" their organization might have. A brainstorming session was used to identify methods and means to continue leadership development outside the class to close the gaps that were discovered.

Reliability and Validity of the Instrument

When tested in the field, over 2,250 survey forms were received; of these 2,239 were useable. The Cronbach's Alpha Index of Reliability was .786080.

Resources

Barksdale, S., & Lund, T. (2001). *Rapid strategic planning*. Alexandria, VA: ASTD.

Barnett, R. (2002). *Winning your way: Character-centered leadership*. Provo, UT: Executive Excellence.

Darden Graduate School of Business Administration at www.darden.virginia.edu/olsson

Goleman, D., Boyatzis, R., & McKee, A. (2004). *Primal leadership*. Cambridge, MA: Harvard Business School Press.

Harvard's John F. Kennedy School of Government at ksgwww.Harvard.edu

Lorsch, J. (2003). *Back to the drawing board: Design corporate boards for a complex world*. Cambridge, MA: Harvard Business School Press.

Parker, J. (2000). *Handbook of emotional intelligence*. San Francisco, CA: Jossey-Bass.

Raelin, J. (2003). *Creating leaderful organizations: How to bring out leadership in everyone*. San Francisco, CA: Berrett-Koehler.

Storey, J. (2004). *Leadership in organizations: Current issues and key trends*. London: Routledge.

Wharton School of Business at www.upenn.edu and knowledge@Wharton.upenn.edu

Teri B. Lund *has been a consultant for fourteen years. Previously she held management positions for Barclays Bank and Kaiser Permanente. She has a bachelor of science degree from Montana State University and a master's in international business and finance from New York University. Ms. Lund has in-depth experience in providing competency solutions for and evaluating the impact of succession planning programs. She is a recognized leader in the area of technology and its impact on learning and performance improvement.*

Leadership Capability Assessment: Self–Assessment

Teri B. Lund

Name: _____ Date: _____

Please list any leadership training you have had in the past five years, the sponsoring organization, and approximate date of the training.

Leadership Program	Sponsoring Organization	Date Attended

Please return this survey to: _____

By (Date): _____

You will receive a summary of this survey in approximately thirty days and any recommended follow-up development opportunities as a result of the information provided.

Instructions: Respond to each question using your first impression. Respond as to how you *most often* respond, not as how you would like to be seen. This information is for developmental purposes and will be used to assist you in further developing your leadership skills to maximize your potential.

Strongly Disagree (1)   Disagree (2)   Neutral (0)   Agree (4)   Strongly Agree (5)

Begin each statement with: "I . . ."

Area 1: Core Skills

Decision Making

Gather information necessary to make a decision through a variety of data collection methods.	1	2	0	4	5
Anticipate the impact the decision will have on other parties.	1	2	0	4	5
Communicate decisions and involve others as appropriate.	1	2	0	4	5

People Management

Listen to others before responding.	1	2	0	4	5
Take responsibility to resolve difficult situations with others effectively.	1	2	0	4	5
Actively contribute to development of others' skills.	1	2	0	4	5

Cross-Organizational Management

Network with others to exchange information.	1	2	0	4	5
Am able to gain consensus from a diverse group.	1	2	0	4	5
Understand the organization's informal structures.	1	2	0	4	5

Process Management

Define objectives for a process in terms of results and new process attributes.	1	2	0	4	5
Define process improvement specifications.	1	2	0	4	5
Interact with individuals across and external to the organization to assist process improvement.	1	2	0	4	5

Strongly Disagree (1)   Disagree (2)   Neutral (0)   Agree (4)   Strongly Agree (5)

Facilitate Change

Proactively identify the need to change by keeping abreast of organizational and competitive information.	1	2	0	4	5
Deal with ambiguity and act without having the total picture.	1	2	0	4	5
Handle risk and uncertainty and aid others in doing the same.	1	2	0	4	5

Comments Regarding Area 1: Core Skills

Area 2: Emotional Intelligence

Initiative

Exhibit a readiness to embark on new ventures.	1	2	0	4	5
Execute actions directed toward new goals.	1	2	0	4	5
Identify opportunities to act on the offensive against competition.	1	2	0	4	5

Affiliation

Volunteer to help others.	1	2	0	4	5
Associate and partner with others inside and external to the organization to complete projects.	1	2	0	4	5
Demonstrate sympathy for others when appropriate.	1	2	0	4	5

Logic Ability

Exhibit intrinsic ability to integrate those who design solutions with those who will build the solutions.	1	2	0	4	5
Extract quantitative data from a given situation.	1	2	0	4	5
Translate available data into various modes and make logical deductions and reasonable conclusions.	1	2	0	4	5

Strongly Disagree (1)   Disagree (2)   Neutral (0)   Agree (4)   Strongly Agree (5)

Power

Demonstrate respect for others.	1	2	0	4	5
Anticipate and avoid unproductive conflict.	1	2	0	4	5
Act honestly and with directness when dealing with personal issues.	1	2	0	4	5

Personal Effectiveness

Use time and resources wisely.	1	2	0	4	5
Am able to work on more than one concept or problem at a time.	1	2	0	4	5
Manage a balance between work and my personal life.	1	2	0	4	5

Comments Regarding Area 2: Emotional Intelligence

Area 3: Strategic Planning and Execution

Global Awareness

Identify potential risk and business impact of changes in global economics or political structure.	1	2	0	4	5
Accept and practice awareness of different country and cultural protocols and values.	1	2	0	4	5
Limit financial and translation or localization exposure when possible.	1	2	0	4	5

Translate Strategy

Develop a plan with resources/dependencies clearly stated.	1	2	0	4	5

Strongly Disagree (1)   Disagree (2)   Neutral (0)   Agree (4)   Strongly Agree (5)

Explain the objectives of the strategic plan as concrete and doable goals.	1	2	0	4	5
Provide foresight into how the business is changing and how the organization needs to react.	1	2	0	4	5

Promoting Organizational Value

Develop higher value products and services for customers.	1	2	0	4	5
Identify ways to increase operational effectiveness.	1	2	0	4	5
Strengthen individual and organizational leadership in the community.	1	2	0	4	5

Financial Management

Predict future revenues or business conditions on the basis of available data.	1	2	0	4	5
Create "what if" scenarios for financial planning purposes.	1	2	0	4	5
Weigh financial criteria when making decisions by placing appropriate emphasis on cost/revenues.	1	2	0	4	5

Entrepreneurship

Analyze situations to make decisions for future business opportunities.	1	2	0	4	5
Create and present concept and product tests or prototypes to gain feedback from audiences.	1	2	0	4	5
Nurture growth and change by leveraging risk and results.	1	2	0	4	5

Comments Regarding Area 3: Strategic Planning and Execution

Leadership Capability Assessment: Observer

Teri B. Lund

Your Name: _____ Date: _____

Person Being Assessed: _____

Please briefly describe your relationship to the leader for whom you are providing feedback.

Please return this form by (Date): _____

To: _____

Instructions: Respond to each question using your first impression. Respond as to how the leader you are providing feedback for most often responds. This information is for developmental purposes and will be used to assist the leader in further developing leadership skills to maximize his or her potential. Results will be anonymous.

Strongly Disagree (1)   **Disagree (2)**   **Neutral (0)**   **Agree (4)**   **Strongly Agree (5)**

Begin each statement with: "This leader . . ."

Area 1: Core Skills

Decision Making

Gathers information necessary to make a decision through a variety of data-collection methods.	1	2	0	4	5
Anticipates the impact that his or her decisions will have on other parties.	1	2	0	4	5
Communicates decisions and involves others as appropriate.	1	2	0	4	5

People Management

Listens to others before responding.	1	2	0	4	5
Takes responsibility for resolving difficult situations with others effectively.	1	2	0	4	5
Actively contributes to development of others' skills.	1	2	0	4	5

Cross-Organizational Management

Networks with others to exchange information.	1	2	0	4	5
Is able to gain consensus from a diverse group.	1	2	0	4	5
Understands the organization's informal structures.	1	2	0	4	5

Process Management

Defines objectives for a process in terms of results and new process attributes.	1	2	0	4	5
Defines process improvement specifications.	1	2	0	4	5
Interacts with individuals across and external to the organization to assist in process improvement.	1	2	0	4	5

Strongly Disagree (1)   Disagree (2)   Neutral (0)   Agree (4)   Strongly Agree (5)

Facilitates Change

Proactively identifies the need to change by keeping
abreast of organizational and competitive information.   1   2   0   4   5

Deals with ambiguity and acts without having the
total picture.   1   2   0   4   5

Handles risk and uncertainty and aids others in
doing the same.   1   2   0   4   5

Comments Regarding Area 1: Core Skills

Area 2: Emotional Intelligence

Initiative

Exhibits a readiness to embark on new ventures.   1   2   0   4   5

Executes actions directed toward new goals.   1   2   0   4   5

Identifies opportunities to act on the offensive
against competition.   1   2   0   4   5

Affiliation

Volunteers to help others.   1   2   0   4   5

Associates and partners with others inside and
external to the organization to complete projects.   1   2   0   4   5

Demonstrates sympathy with others when
appropriate.   1   2   0   4   5

Logic Ability

Exhibits intrinsic ability to integrate those who design
solutions with those who will build the solutions.   1   2   0   4   5

Extracts quantitative data from a given situation.   1   2   0   4   5

Translates available data into various modes and
makes logical deductions and reasonable conclusions.   1   2   0   4   5

Strongly Disagree (1)   Disagree (2)   Neutral (0)   Agree (4)   Strongly Agree (5)

Power

Demonstrates respect for others.	1	2	0	4	5
Anticipates and avoids unproductive conflict.	1	2	0	4	5
Acts honestly and with directness when dealing with personal issues.	1	2	0	4	5

Personal Effectiveness

Uses time and resources wisely.	1	2	0	4	5
Is able to work on more than one concept or problem at a time.	1	2	0	4	5
Manages to balance his or her work and personal lives.	1	2	0	4	5

Comments Regarding Area 2: Emotional Intelligence

Area 3: Strategic Planning and Execution

Global Awareness

Identifies potential risk and business impact of changes in global economies or political structures.	1	2	0	4	5
Accepts and practices awareness of different country and cultural protocols and values.	1	2	0	4	5
Limits financial and translation or localization exposure when possible.	1	2	0	4	5

Translates Strategy

Develops plans with resources/dependencies clearly stated.	1	2	0	4	5
Explains the objectives of the strategic plan as concrete and doable goals.	1	2	0	4	5

Strongly Disagree (1)   Disagree (2)   Neutral (0)   Agree (4)   Strongly Agree (5)

Has foresight about how business is changing and
how the organization needs to react.   1   2   0   4   5

Promoting Organizational Value

Develops higher value products and services for
customer.   1   2   0   4   5

Identifies ways to increase operational effectiveness.   1   2   0   4   5

Strengthens individual and organizational leadership
in community.   1   2   0   4   5

Financial Management

Predicts future revenues or business conditions on
basis of available data.   1   2   0   4   5

Creates "what if" scenarios for financial planning
purposes.   1   2   0   4   5

Weighs a financial criterion when making decisions
by placing appropriate emphasis on cost/revenues.   1   2   0   4   5

Entrepreneurship

Analyzes situations to make decisions for future
business opportunities.   1   2   0   4   5

Creates and presents concept and product tests or
prototypes to gain feedback from audiences.   1   2   0   4   5

Nurtures growth and change by leveraging risk
and results.   1   2   0   4   5

Comments Regarding Area 3: Strategic Planning and Execution

Scoring Sheet

Instructions: Use the following instructions to calculate each leader's Self and Observer scores from the Leadership Capability Assessment.

Transfer the self-scores into the rule after Leader's Self-Scores. For the other scores or "feedback" scores, calculate an average by adding the scores for each item together and dividing by the number of those providing feedback to that leader. Place this number on the Feedback Average line.

Consolidate the themes of the comments in each of the Area comment areas for that leader.

Note: You may use this same scoring sheet to analyze the average of all leaders you surveyed. To accomplish this, add the leadership scores together for each item and divide by the number of leaders. Average those providing feedback as well. This will provide you a view of the strengths and weaknesses for the group of leaders you surveyed.

Area 1: Core Skills

Leader Self-Score: _____

Feedback Average Score: _____

Decision Making

Gathers information necessary to make a decision through a variety of data collection methods.

Anticipates the impact the decision will have on other parties.

Communicates decisions and involves others as appropriate.

People Management

Listens to others before responding.

Takes responsibility to resolve difficult situations with others effectively.

Actively contributes to development of others' skills.

Cross-Organizational Management

Networks with others to exchange information.

Able to gain consensus from a diverse group.

Understands organization's informal structures.

Process Management

>   Defines objectives for a process in terms of results and new process attributes.

>   Defines process improvement specifications.

>   Interacts with individuals across and external to the organization to assist process improvement.

Facilitates Change

>   Proactively identifies the need to change by keeping abreast of organizational and competitive information.

>   Deals with ambiguity and acts without having the total picture.

>   Handles risk and uncertainty and aids others in doing the same.

Comments Regarding Area 1: Core Skills

Area 2: Emotional Intelligence

Leader Self-Score: _____

Feedback Average Score: _____

Initiative

>   Exhibits a readiness to embark on new ventures.

>   Executes actions directed toward new goals.

>   Identifies opportunities to act on offensive in competition.

Affiliation

>   Volunteers to help others.

>   Associates and partners with others inside and external to the organization to complete projects.

>   Demonstrates sympathy to others when appropriate.

Logic Ability

Exhibits intrinsic ability to integrate those who design solutions with those who will build the solutions.

Extracts quantitative data from a given situation.

Translates available data into various modes and makes logical deductions and reasonable conclusions.

Power

Demonstrates respect for others.

Anticipates and avoids unproductive conflict.

Acts honestly and with directness when dealing with personal issues.

Personal Effectiveness

Uses time and resources wisely.

Able to work on more than one concept or problem at a time.

Balances work and personal lives.

Comments Regarding Area 2: Emotional Intelligence

Area 3: Strategic Planning and Execution

Leader Self-Score: _____

Feedback Average Score: _____

Global Awareness

Identifies potential risk and business impact of change in global economics or political structure.

Accepts and practices awareness of different country and cultural protocols and values.

Limits financial and translation or localization exposure when possible.

Translates Strategy

Develops a plan with resources/dependencies clearly stated.

Explains the objectives of the strategic plan in terms of concrete and doable goals.

Provides foresight into how business is changing and organization needs to react.

Promotes Organization Value

Develops higher value products and services for customer.

Identifies ways to increase operational effectiveness.

Strengthens individual and organizational leadership in community.

Financial Management

Predicts future revenues or business conditions on basis of available data.

Creates "what if" scenarios for financial planning purposes.

Weighs financial criteria when making decisions by placing appropriate emphasis on cost/revenues.

Entrepreneurship

Analyzes situations to make decisions for future business opportunities.

Creates and presents concept and product tests or prototypes to gain feedback from audiences.

Nurtures growth and change by leveraging risk and results.

Comments Regarding Area 3: Strategic Planing and Execution

Analysis Questions

In viewing the data, consider the following questions:

1. Is there an area for which the scores were on average lower than the other two areas? For example, on average was the Emotional Intelligence area scored lower than the other two?

2. Is there consistency in the scoring in a category such as Decision Making across leaders or those providing feedback? For example, does the leader score him/herself higher in "Anticipating the impact the decision will have on other parties," than those who provide feedback score him/her?

3. Are the leader's self scores consistently higher than those that were provided by those who were giving feedback? Or were there areas where the leader's score was lower?

4. Is there consistency in the level of all the leaders' scores? For example a senior leader may score herself higher in Strategic Planning than someone who is in a Succession Planning Program scored himself.

5. Is there consistency across the scores by the type of individuals providing feedback? For example, peers score the leader lower and associates score the leader higher.

6. Is there an item, category, or area that is consistently lower across leaders in your organization?

Motivational Climate Inventory

K.S. Gupta

Summary

What motivates employees is a very old, but still unanswered question. The rapid changes in the economic and social environment in the 21st century have made this question even more important, as well as more complex for practicing managers to answer. The answer lies somewhere in the motivational climate of organizations.

This scale was developed to examine the relationship between motivational climate of organizations and intrinsic motivation of junior and mid-level executives in manufacturing, service, and information technology organizations. A highly motivating climate ultimately results in certain positive outcomes.

The process of globalization has resulted, among other things, in changed market conditions and high competition. An industry can no longer count either on captive markets or on protection from government regulation. In the new market economy, the philosophy of survival of the fittest is gradually replacing the planned and regulated economy. The transition from old order to new order is accompanied by both uncertainty and pain for captains of industry and for industrial workers.

An organization's culture is developed through concentrated efforts. These efforts result in new policies, practices, procedures, and routines and to shared beliefs and values, all of which contribute to high performance of an organization.

Organizational Climate

Organizational climate is perceived in many different ways. The variables of the "right" motivational climate are shown in Figure 1. It can be defined as:

- How customers feel during any or all of their relationships with the organization;

- The attitudes of employees that affect their behavior toward customers (both internal and external);

- The feelings of people about an organization, both inside and outside;

- All the factors influencing employee satisfaction, their interpersonal relationships, their communication, shared values and goals, and their levels of responsibility and participation in the functioning of the organization;

- The feelings of employee about management and their relationships with peers and subordinates; and

- Employees' feelings about the work environment and, therefore, how they function in their jobs in relation to their managers, their peers, and their customers.

Work Motivation

The question as to what motivates an employee continues to challenge the imagination of academicians and practitioners alike. For more than half a century, social scientists and thinkers have devoted much time and energy to the subject and have come up with many different models and hypotheses to explain what motivates employees.

The best answer is that motivation is multi-faceted. An employee may enjoy the work assigned to him but may not like the organization he is working for, or vice versa. Similarly a person may be very happy with the organization but may find the interpersonal/inter-group climate to be frustrating. Human nature can be very simple, yet very complex. An understanding and appreciation of this is a prerequisite to effectively motivating employees in the workplace—and therefore effective management and leadership.

The practical aspects of motivation in the workplace have been explored, and much research has been undertaken in the field, notably by Douglas McGregor (Theory Y), Frederick Herzberg (two-factor motivation hygiene theory), Abraham Maslow (theory z, hierarchy of needs), Elton Mayo (Hawthorne experiments), and Chris Argyris, Rensis Likert, and David McClelland (achievement motivation).

The Key to Performance Improvement

There is an old saying that you can take a horse to water but you cannot force it to drink. So it is with people. They will do what they want to do or are otherwise motivated to do. Whether it is to excel on the factory floor or in the "ivory tower," they must be motivated or driven to it, either by internal or external stimuli. Are people born with the self-motivation or drive? Self-motivation is a learned skill. If someone does not have it, he or she still can be motivated by external rewards. Learning what motivates their people is essential for any business that wants to survive and succeed. Performance can be described as a function of ability and motivation, thus:

$$\text{Job Performance} = f(\text{ability})(\text{motivation})$$

Ability depends on education, experience, and training. Improving employees' abilities is a long, slow process. On the other hand motivation can be improved quickly.

The Employee Motivational Climate Inventory

The inventory was developed to study motivational parameters, along with the outcomes and effect of using them to influence employees.

A number of studies indicate that the organizational climate should provide time for enjoyable work, as this is motivating for employees and helps to keep them at a job and to perform better.

The framework we have developed to outline motivational climate contains ten variables. These are

- Adaptability
- Transparency
- Positive feedback
- Respect for employees
- Developing employees
- Encouraging innovation
- Appreciation
- Punctuality
- Role modeling
- Autonomy

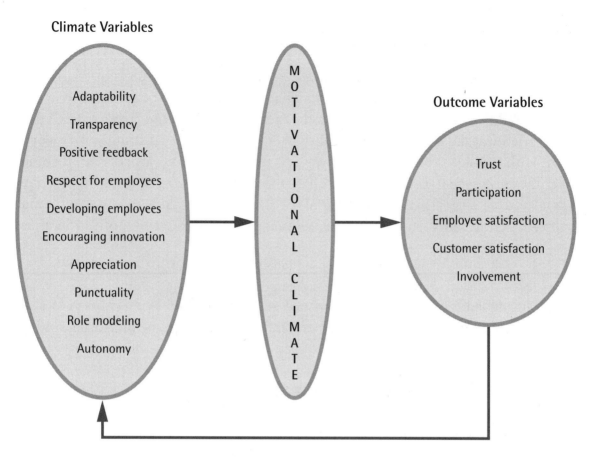

Figure 1.   Framework for Motivational Climate

When there was a good motivational climate, that is, scores were high in the ten variables above, we found there to be five outcome variables. These were

- Trust

- Participation

- Employee satisfaction

- Customer satisfaction

- Involvement

Methodology

Data were collected by the author while conducting training workshops for various organizations on a variety of topics of interest to these organizations in the soft skills development area. The respondents were 570 junior and mid-level managers (490 males and 80 females) from manufacturing, services, and IT areas. Their ages ranged from 23 to 47.

During the workshops, the original inventory of 78 items was administered. The first 250 samples were factor analyzed. Factor loadings of more than 0.5 were considered to develop a stronger scale. The modified inventory contains 60 items.

Reliability and Validity

The validity was ascertained by the test-retest method. Validity was found to be 0.9038. The internal consistency varied from 0.9132 to 0.9247. The alpha value for 570 respondents was 0.9128.

Utility of the Instrument

The instrument provides a measurement of motivation variables from 1 to 5. An average value less than 3.0 was found to contribute to a poor motivational climate. The average score for the total survey and also the individual items should not be less than 3.0. If it is, there is a serious problem in the organization that calls for an urgent intervention. The manager of a function with low scores should focus attention on the low-scoring variables and bring about the desired change through suitable interventions.

Suggested Uses and Interpretations

After administering the survey to the target group in any organization, the trainer can score the inventory by averaging, as shown on the scoring sheet. The trainer can help the manager to select the interventions most likely to result in the desired change. The inventory can be taken again at a later date in order to quantify results and change that has taken place.

References

Herzberg, F., Mausner, B., & Snyderman, B. (1959). *The motivation to work.* New York: John Wiley & Sons.

Maslow, A. (1954). *Motivation and personality.* New York: Harper & Row.

Mayo, E. (1933). *The human problems of an industrial civilization.* New York: Macmillan.

McClelland, D.C. (1961). *The achieving society.* New York: Van Nostrand Reinhold.

McGregor, D. (1960). *The human side of enterprise.* New York: McGraw-Hill.

Dr. K.S. Gupta, *senior faculty in HAL Management Academy, Vimanapura, Bangalore-560017, India, holds a master's degree in electronics engineering, an MBA specializing in HR and marketing, and a doctorate in management from the Indian Institute of Technology, Mumbai, India.*

His thirty-three years of experience cover the areas of aircraft maintenance, overhauling of aircraft and accessories, quality assurance and airworthiness, plant maintenance, international marketing, faculty in technical and management disciplines, guide for Ph.D., ME, and MBA scholars, and training and consultancy. He has served as faculty in technical and management areas.

He has presented/published twenty-five papers, among them The Empowerment Inventory, published by Pfeiffer in the 2002 Consulting Annual *and Measuring a Child's Empowerment in the* 2004 Training Annual.

Motivational Climate Inventory

K.S. Gupta

Instructions: The following inventory consists of sixty items reflecting your perceptions of the motivational climate in your organization. Circle the response you feel is appropriate for each of the items:

1 = **Never true**   2 = **Sometimes true**   3 = **True relatively often**
4 = **Often true**   5 = **Very often true**

1.	The top management of this organization believes that human resources are extremely important and that people have to be treated humanely.	1	2	3	4	5
2.	Superiors praise the good work done by employees in public.	1	2	3	4	5
3.	Bosses set high goals for themselves.	1	2	3	4	5
4.	I make all my own decisions about my area of work.	1	2	3	4	5
5.	I receive necessary information in time to carry out my work efficiently.	1	2	3	4	5
6.	This organization facilitates and provides opportunities for individuals to do creative work.	1	2	3	4	5
7.	I am satisfied with my career progress in this organization.	1	2	3	4	5
8.	Bosses here treat subordinates as a vital resource for gaining competitive advantage.	1	2	3	4	5
9.	Meetings generally start on time.	1	2	3	4	5
10.	Problems between departments are generally resolved through mutual effort and understanding.	1	2	3	4	5
11.	I feel that I am responsible for whatever happens to my organization, whether good or bad.	1	2	3	4	5
12.	Communication within this organization is very open.	1	2	3	4	5

1 = Never true   2 = Sometimes true   3 = True relatively often
4 = Often true   5 = Very often true

13. People in my organization solve their work-related
    problems with mutual discussions.   1   2   3   4   5

14. My organization facilitates employee self-
    improvement.   1   2   3   4   5

15. This organization is receptive to new ideas.   1   2   3   4   5

16. I receive regular feedback on my work performance.   1   2   3   4   5

17. Any weaknesses are communicated to employees
    in a non-threatening way.   1   2   3   4   5

18. Employees are sponsored for training on the basis
    of genuine training needs.   1   2   3   4   5

19. Bosses here generally go to subordinates to
    express appreciation for a job well done.   1   2   3   4   5

20. Superiors hold themselves to high ethical standards.   1   2   3   4   5

21. People here have an opportunity to develop their
    job skills further.   1   2   3   4   5

22. I am satisfied with my job.   1   2   3   4   5

23. It is easy to ask for advice from anyone in my
    organization.   1   2   3   4   5

24. My boss asks for my views before making
    decisions about my work.   1   2   3   4   5

25. Superiors invite their subordinates to discuss
    their work.   1   2   3   4   5

26. Suggestions are encouraged and suitably rewarded.   1   2   3   4   5

27. Everyone in the organization contributes to
    waste reduction.   1   2   3   4   5

28. Employees returning from training programs are
    given opportunities to try out what they learned.   1   2   3   4   5

29. Operating procedures are used as guidelines and
    may not be followed strictly at all times.   1   2   3   4   5

1 = Never true   2 = Sometimes true   3 = True relatively often

4 = Often true   5 = Very often true

30.	Everyone has a chance to express opinions on how to do the work.	1	2	3	4	5
31.	I care about the growth of this organization.	1	2	3	4	5
32.	I allow my subordinates to make their own decisions while carrying out their work.	1	2	3	4	5
33.	I am willing to devote my free time to work.	1	2	3	4	5
34.	Bosses do not blame others for problems.	1	2	3	4	5
35.	I am satisfied with the people in my work group.	1	2	3	4	5
36.	My organization is flexible enough to adopt to any change quickly.	1	2	3	4	5
37.	My organization encourages innovation.	1	2	3	4	5
38.	Top management encourages new ideas and risk taking.	1	2	3	4	5
39.	Bosses ensure that their people have the training they require.	1	2	3	4	5
40.	People here easily learn new technology required for new product development.	1	2	3	4	5
41.	People here generally maintain the schedule of supplying the needs of both internal and external customers.	1	2	3	4	5
42.	People here generally stand by their commitments.	1	2	3	4	5
43.	While away from the job, I often worry that my work is suffering.	1	2	3	4	5
44.	Organizational policies support the ability to speed up the work.	1	2	3	4	5
45.	Bosses here are conscious about the value of others' time.	1	2	3	4	5
46.	Superiors help employees in setting higher goals.	1	2	3	4	5

1 = Never true   2 = Sometimes true   3 = True relatively often
4 = Often true   5 = Very often true

47. Bosses here go to subordinates to exchange
    information.   1   2   3   4   5

48. People here believe that internal customer satisfac-
    tion is essential for external customer satisfaction.   1   2   3   4   5

49. Celebrations of achievements are common here.   1   2   3   4   5

50. Here bosses normally do what they say and they
    say what they do.   1   2   3   4   5

51. I am satisfied with my superior.   1   2   3   4   5

52. Both internal and external customers appreciate
    our work.   1   2   3   4   5

53. My colleagues share their views before any
    decisions are made on work issues.   1   2   3   4   5

54. Here people are making good efforts to reduce
    the cost of product.   1   2   3   4   5

55. People arrive at the office on time.   1   2   3   4   5

56. Superiors participate in training to improve
    their competencies.   1   2   3   4   5

57. Bosses trust their people.   1   2   3   4   5

58. Bosses take responsibility for their part in
    mistakes.   1   2   3   4   5

59. Superiors share their strengths honestly.   1   2   3   4   5

60. In general, employees are satisfied.   1   2   3   4   5

Motivation Climate Scoring Sheet

Instructions: Use the grid below to calculate your scores for each variable. Write the score you assigned to each item in Scores Received column. Add the numbers in each box together and divide by the number of items in that box to obtain an average score. Put this number in the Average Score column.

Climate Variables	Item Numbers	Scores Received	Average Score
Adaptability	29, 36, 40, 44		
Transparency	12, 25, 59		
Positive feedback	5, 16, 17, 49		
Respect for employees	1, 8, 47		
Developing employees	14, 18, 21, 39, 56		
Encouraging innovation	6, 15 28, 37, 38		
Appreciation	2, 19, 26, 52		
Punctuality	9, 41, 45, 55		
Role modeling	3, 34, 58, 62		
Autonomy	4, 24, 32, 53		
Trust	23, 50, 57		
Participation	10,, 13, 30, 46		
Employee satisfaction	7, 22, 35, 43, 51		
Customer satisfaction	27, 42, 48, 54		
Involvement	11, 31, 33, 60		

The 2006 Pfeiffer Annual: Consulting

Introduction
to the Articles and Discussion Resources Section

The Articles and Discussion Resources Section is a collection of materials useful to every facilitator. The theories, background information, models, and methods will challenge facilitators' thinking, enrich their professional development, and assist their internal and external clients with productive change. These articles may be used as a basis for lecturettes, as handouts in training sessions, or as background reading material. This section will provide you with a variety of useful ideas, theoretical opinions, teachable models, practical strategies, and proven intervention methods. The articles will add richness and depth to your training and consulting knowledge and skills. They will challenge you to think differently, explore new concepts, and experiment with new interventions. The articles will continue to add a fresh perspective to your work.

The 2006 Pfeiffer Annual: Consulting includes eleven articles, in the following categories:

Communication: Clarity and Precision in Communication

Turning Reports into Successful Oral Presentations, by Nichola D. Gutgold

Communication: Coaching and Encouraging

Why Executive Coaching? Significant Lessons Learned, by Barbara Pate Glacel

Problem Solving: Models, Methods, and Techniques

Collaborative Management, by Peter R. Garber

Problem Solving: Change and Change Agents

Results of the Effective Change Survey, by Rick Maurer

Groups and Teams: Team Building and Team Development

Teams of a New Generation: Defining the 21st Century Experiential Training Agenda, by Greg Robinson and Mark Rose

Consulting/Training: OD Theory and Practice

A Coaching Challenge: Surviving the Arrogant Boss, by H.B. Karp

Consulting/Training: Strategies and Techniques

Inside or Outside: The Partnerships of Internal and External Consultants, by Beverly Scott and Jane Hascall

Consulting/Training: Interface with Clients

Making a Difference: The Client-Consultant Relationship, by Mohandas K. Nair

Facilitating: Techniques and Strategies

Accelerating the Project Lifecycle: The Partnership of Facilitation and Project Management, by Tammy Adams and Jan Means

Leadership: Strategies and Techniques

Giving Feedback to Leaders: Avoiding the Traps, by Jan M. Schmuckler and Thomas J. Ucko

Leadership: Top-Management Issues and Concerns

How to Persuade Employees to Buy In to Change, by Charles B. Royal

As with previous *Annuals,* this volume covers a wide variety of topics. The range of articles presented encourages thought-provoking discussion about the present and future of HRD. We have done our best to categorize the articles for easy reference; however, many of the articles encompass a range of topics, disciplines, and applications. If you do not find what you are looking for under one category, check a related category. In some cases we may place an article in the "Training" *Annual* that also has implications for "Consulting" and vice versa. As the field of HRD continues to grow and develop, there is more and more crossover between training and consulting. Explore all the contents of both volumes of the *Annual* in order to realize the full potential for learning and development that each offers.

Turning Reports into Successful Oral Presentations

Nichola D. Gutgold

Summary

The world of work requires effective communicators. But each day careers are sidetracked and messages are bungled by the inability of professionals to deliver written work in a compelling way. Some of the confusion may center around the differences between public speaking and paper presentations. Public speaking is more theatrical, reserved for more formal events, such as political speeches, keynote business addresses, and even toasts at a wedding. Paper presentations, on the other hand, require the speaker to make points in an oral context, not a written one, and to do so with precision and flair. By following the guidelines in this article, business professionals and scholars who present their work at conferences will gain insight into striking the right balance between oral communication that compels the audience to listen and making sure that the audience receives the full message.

If you have been in the audience at a business meeting where a colleague is delivering a paper, you know all too well how boring it is to listen to a written report being read aloud. However, workers want to be sure to communicate the most salient issues of the paper; therefore, they are reluctant to speak more informally. That is why this article is of value to anyone in an organization who needs to deliver a paper presentation. Delivering a paper is not the same as giving a public speech.

A search of many basic public speaking textbooks, organizational communication textbooks, and even professional speaking books geared to businesspeople will find that the authors use the terms "presentation" and "speech" interchangeably. In most basic public speaking textbooks, techniques for delivering a paper at a professional conference or in a classroom are not even considered. While *Presentations in Everyday Life* promises, by its title, to include practical public speaking advice, nowhere in the text are paper presentation techniques offered (Daly & Engleberg, 2001). The best-selling basic public speaking textbook in the country, Stephen Lucas' (2004) *The Art of Public Speaking,* completely ignores the subject of paper presentations. In *Fundamentals of Organizational Communication: Knowledge, Sensitivity, Skills and Values,* the term "presentational speaking" is used to describe both public speeches and technical report delivery (Shockley-Zalabak, 2002, p. 296). In the late 1990s, Penn State University made a university-wide change in the name of the basic speech course from "Effective Speech" to "Effective Presentations," yet the course content remained the same.

Yet, when our colleagues or we present scholarly work at a conference or in a meeting, the purpose and presentation style differ from a traditional public speech in several important ways. Business professionals are frequently asked to share reports with staff, and still there is a lack of advice available to help them turn their written pages into effective oral presentations.

In this article I will offer suggestions for giving successful scholarly or business presentations. I refer to them as "talks" or presentations, which I differentiate from the more theatrical form of public speech that we are likely to encounter in other public settings, such as politics, graduation ceremonies, weddings, and during business dinner speeches.

A good talk will not conceal poor scholarship, but a poor one could negate even a very good research effort. A scholarly presentation consists of two parts: (1) the information that you wish to tell the audience and (2) the information that you want to show the audience. You may wish to show graphs, charts, photos, or even objects to more clearly make a point about your scholarship.

To "speak" a paper, you should define a few critical messages that you want the audience to take away from the presentation. In many cases, this requires significant editing, since scholarly papers usually have a significant amount of detail that is not easily reduced to a few points. For this reason, scholars should always provide copies of their papers for the audience to read after the presentation. It is important, however, that you not read your paper. Written language use and oral language use are different, and audiences become bored when being read a scholarly paper. Also, it is unlikely that you can cover everything written in the typical amount of time granted a speaker. Therefore, you will want to focus a talk differently than the way a paper is focused.

Focusing Listeners' Attention

You should "signpost," that is, use verbal markers to indicate important points in the presentation or argument. "Signposts" include such verbal indicators as transitions, internal summaries, and previews. A transition is also known as a connective, since it literally connects one point in the presentation to another. Common transitions are italicized in the following sentences:

- *In addition* to being an excellent singer, Joni Mitchell has gained acclaim as an artist.

- Pundits say that the spouse of a candidate doesn't have an impact in the polls, *yet* popular first ladies are used excessively on the campaign trail.

- *Of equal importance* is following up with a phone call when you want to stress your interest in a position.

- *On the other hand,* those students who work and attend classes are more mature than those who simply attend school.

- *Finally,* when selecting a job candidate, remember that manners matter!

Internal previews reveal or suggest salient points in your presentation. They tell the audience what you are going to cover and in what order. For example:

> What is Robert Kennedy's legacy? Some say he is a martyr like his brother, John, and others say he was just another case of nepotism. Either or both perceptions of his life shape his legacy.

Internal summaries are similar to internal previews, except that a summary *ends* a section, whereas a preview *begins* one. Here's how the presentation on Robert Kennedy would benefit from an internal summary:

> Remember that the legacy of Robert Kennedy is influenced by two schools of thought: one that he was a martyr who died advocating his beliefs and another that he was an overrated politician whose quick rise was due to one factor: family influence.

The academic paper on Robert Kennedy would contain many more details. However, for an oral presentation, simplicity is key. Being redundant is encouraged when delivering a scholarly paper, since both simplicity and some redundancy can help listeners to remember the most salient points of your presentation.

What to Say and When to Say It

A Presentation Outline

What follows is an outline for presenting a research paper. Depending on the discipline, some information will change; however, this offers you a guide to follow that will ensure a thorough and engaging presentation that meets your needs as well as those of your audience.

I. The Thesis Clearly Stated in a Method That Provokes Thinking

Create listener interest by beginning with a question, short story, quotation, or striking statement. There are several questions that you should consider answering at this beginning phase. What is the thesis? Why should the author or the audience care about it?

II. The Contributions of This Paper

Having clearly described the thesis in a way that creates audience interest in the subject, next describe the specific study and approach of the paper. If it is theoretical, offer an overview of the techniques, setting, model, and the main results. If it is empirical or experimental, describe the model or hypotheses to be tested, the data set or experimental design, and the methodology used to analyze the data. Clarity and brevity are important, even if the audience is well schooled in the subject, because a talk is meant to be less detailed than the written document.

III. Relationship to the Literature

Put the contribution of the paper in perspective by describing how the results of the paper fit with what is already known.

IV. Definitions and Descriptions of Data

Convey the basic insights and intuitions of the paper.

V. Main Results

Remember to focus on information that will help the audience understand your research and its most salient features.

VI. Conclusions

Present implications for future research as well as the limitations of the results. Just as in the beginning of the talk, sum up dramatically and with attention to the needs of the audience.

Even more precisely, here is a four-step set of features for presenting scholarly work to an audience:

1. Engage the listeners with the thesis of the study.

2. Explain your methodology or why you researched this topic.

3. Share your findings.

4. Concisely offer conclusions and opportunities for future research in a way that sums up your topic and creates audience interest.

Responding to Questions

You should encourage discussion, since it is the main function of most scholarly presentations. Once discussion ensues, how to handle audience questions is also an important feature of scholarly paper presentations. Welcome questions and patiently listen to the question without stepping on the questioner's words. Pausing and not rushing the answer is also important, since it shows that you are listening carefully to the question. Repeat the question into the microphone, if there is one, so that everyone in the room knows what it is, and answer only the question that has been asked—no more and no less. Make eye contact with the entire audience, not just with the person who has asked the question.

If you have been asked to present your paper for twenty minutes, ask how much total time you will have, since you will want to save at least 20 percent of your talk for questions and audience interaction and discussion.

Using Visuals

If you wish to include visuals in a presentation, there are a few rules to follow. First, keep them simple! PowerPoint® is a great tool, but the focus of the presentation should still be on you, not on fancy computer graphics. Overheads are just as effective as PowerPoint and tend to distract less from the speaker. Overheads or PowerPoint can serve the purpose of helping you keep yourself "on point." They will allow you to move around a bit and create a more natural effect than if you are simply glued to the podium.

Also, overheads or PowerPoint slides that contain graphs or tables help the audience to see what you mean without a complicated oral explanation. Text on overheads or on PowerPoint should be large enough so that the entire audience can read it without straining (at least 24 points). Limiting text on overheads or PowerPoint to bulleted items will further simplify and clarify the message.

Conclusion

The main goal of a good research presentation is to present your research in an engaging and relevant manner. It is likely that your audience will contain a world expert on your topic as well as people who have never even heard of your topic. Your challenge is to make the material equally understandable and interesting to both audiences.

References

Daly, J., & Engleberg, I. (2001). *Presentations in everyday life.* Boston, MA: Houghton-Mifflin.

Lucas, S. (2004). *The art of public speaking.* New York: McGraw-Hill.

Shockley-Zalabak, P. (2002). *Fundamentals of organizational communication: Knowledge, sensitivity, skills and values.* Boston, MA: Allyn and Bacon.

Nichola D. Gutgold, *Ph.D., has been teaching public speaking for more than fifteen years. Dr. Gutgold is an assistant professor of Communication, Arts, and Sciences at Penn State Berks-Lehigh Valley College, where she is also the co-director of Communication Across the Curriculum. She holds a bachelor of arts in communications and English from King's College, a master's degree in speech communication from Bloomsburg University of Pennsylvania, and a Ph.D. in speech communication from Pennsylvania State University. She is co-author (with Elizabeth Hanford Dole) of* Speaking from the Heart *(Praeger Press, 2004) and author of numerous articles and chapters. Her two main areas of research are women's rhetoric and pedagogy of public speaking.*

Why Executive Coaching?
Significant Lessons Learned

Barbara Pate Glacel

Summary

Executive coaching is a popular technique for improving the performance and job satisfaction of successful leaders. To benefit from coaching, executives must be open to learning about themselves, receiving sometimes-difficult feedback, and making changes to improve their performance and relationships with others.

This article cites examples from a year-long coaching engagement with an already-successful leader who was able to reflect on the benefits of the coaching and the feedback she received. While her lessons learned are particular to her case, there are universal lessons for good leaders about successful performance by organizational executives.

During the past few years, executive coaching has become *de rigueur* for leaders who are good, challenged, motivated, and productive. It is not reserved for those who need to be "fixed." In fact, those executives who are already successful are the ones who benefit the most from executive coaching because they need only improve around the margins. They are aware that no one person is good at everything, so they seek out opportunities to improve themselves, to build on their own good ideas, and to engage in conversations with others who represent diverse points of view.

On the other hand, the executives who engage in coaching to be "fixed" are often the very ones who believe that leaders must have all the answers. They, therefore, are less inclined to be receptive to different points of view. This is an attitude of new managers who somehow have been led to believe that the mantle of "manager" means that the holder of the title must always have the answer. That manager does not know how to ask questions, and, therefore, this limits one's ability to learn.

Executive coaching, at its best, uses a Socratic method of questioning that allows the executive to reflect on behavior, situations, alternatives, and consequences. The questioning opens up various perspectives and options that allow for better solutions to both business and personnel decisions. Only when the executive admits to *not* knowing can the executive learn more about better management and leadership.

Executive coaching relationships are built on both trust and interpersonal chemistry between the coach and the executive. It takes time for this foundation to be built, so most coaching relationships last from six months to two years. During this time, the coach becomes an alter ego with whom the executive can discuss current situations, tactical maneuvers, and strategic decisions that impact the leader, the team, the organization, and the business result. Utilization of a coach in this manner is not a crutch. It is, in fact, the addition of a resource in an executive's toolkit that allows for better decision making.

Lessons Learned

At the end of a year-long coaching assignment, one executive reflected on what she had learned during the previous year. During that year, she had received real-time feedback through her coach based on qualitative responses to interviews with her boss, subordinates, and peers. She took that feedback to heart, deciding what specific actions she could take to improve her leadership and her business results. Her learnings are significant examples of improvement at the margins that have made this already-effective executive even more successful.

Perception Is Reality

The executive reflected, "I was aware of most of the challenges that were reported in the executive assessment feedback. However, I was stunned that I was perceived as too much like a more senior executive who was not well regarded in the company. I needed to work on the perception of others."

The higher one progresses within an organization, the less feedback one receives. Women, throughout their careers, typically receive even less feedback than men receive. So the opportunity to receive feedback through an executive coach may provide a real eye-opener. This executive, in fact, was "stunned" to view herself through the eyes of others. The fact that this executive accepted the feedback and did not become defensive about it enabled her to learn from and deal with the situation. Others' perceptions of her behavior were limiting her effectiveness and her ability to get things accomplished through others. When she understood that the perceptions of others were, in fact, their truth, she could deal with changing those perceptions.

One technique that she used to change their perceptions was the practice of "pre-calling." She began explaining her behavior and her reactions to others before she acted. She allowed them to understand what was going on in her mind and what led her to behave in certain ways. She reached out to others more frequently, particularly those in locations remote from her own. She allowed others to get to know her as a person. All of these efforts began to pay off in changing the negative perception that others had of her.

Trust and Credibility Are the Basis of Business Relationships

The executive observed, "I learned that it is important with a new business to quickly develop a relationship to build trust and credibility. One must do this in the beginning." The feedback she received revealed a problematic relationship with a business unit located 3,000 miles from hers. Their remoteness made relationship building more difficult. The fact that a relationship had not been built in the beginning meant that a poor relationship needed to be repaired. This was even more difficult with a 3,000-mile separation.

During the coaching period, this executive worked very hard to repair the problematic relationship. She began making routine telephone calls to key players to share information. She copied them more often on key reports and memoranda for the record. She included them on conference calls with partners, clients, and suppliers. She learned how to listen first and express her opinions later. This practice demonstrated that she wanted others' input and valued their ideas.

During the same period of time, she was paired with another business unit for the first time, and they were jointly tasked to bring a new product to market. Having learned the lesson that trust and credibility are the basis of good business relationships, she set out from the start to get to know her new colleagues. She purposefully spent time with them, learned their technology, and listened to their goals. She found ways to help them achieve those goals, building both trust and credibility in the relationship.

Common Ground Overcomes Interpersonal Difficulties

Inevitably, disagreements or personality conflicts arise in business relationships. Strong leaders are equally able to create allies and adversaries. However, adversaries may add value, so it may be important to keep them on the same team. This executive reflected, "I no longer avoid people with whom I am uncomfortable. I seek the person out in order to work on bringing down the barriers between us. I reach out to connect to the person with whom I have a problem relationship. It is easier to be tolerant about someone's behavior when I like the person. I get to know people with whom I work so that I can find common ground. Not liking someone raises artificial barriers so that I don't trust their competence."

A key behavior that she learned was the ability to swallow a quick retort when she did not agree. In her words, she learned to "stop and think before I react. I ask myself, 'what is he really telling me?' so that I do not damage the relationship. I try not to be catty or nonprofessional back. I let the person talk, realizing that he is trying to help me out."

In order to improve her relationships with others, she worked to find common ground with those whom she needed to accomplish her work and those who might influence her career. She learned that she could not distance herself from others just because she found them difficult to work with. She had to find a common path and build coalitions with others. Sometimes, in fact, having a common enemy helps to bring together those with problematic relationships.

Blind Spots Matter

When leaders do not receive feedback, they can be excused from not knowing their impact on others or the perception that others have of them. But when they receive feedback and disregard it, they are guilty of having a blind spot and not taking advantage of good feedback. This executive had risen to senior levels of a technical organization because of her outstanding leadership, but she had not paid attention to learning and keeping up with the technical skills of her subordinates.

At senior levels, leaders need fewer technical skills and more leadership skills. However, in technical organizations, they must exhibit knowledge of the technology and its relevance to their work in order to build credibility and to make decisions that have systemic impacts. This executive usually deferred to her technical experts, and, thus, others did not trust her judgment on technical matters. She typically dismissed this criticism as not a problem. Through the coaching, however, she learned: "I need to exhibit the technical knowledge I have and become more technically informed."

This realization was not startling, but it had been in her blind spot for a long time. In fact, her blindness to the situation had kept her from understanding the relationship of her group to others in the company. She reflected, "I have had a blind spot revealed. I didn't recognize my ignorance of some others and their connections to my work. Now, I have expanded my network. I keep my peers more in the loop. Last year, I did not know they were related to me, but my investment in learning the technology has helped me realize the relationships."

To exhibit her understanding, she began making the technical presentations rather than deferring to her technical expert subordinates. This increased the trust that others had in her and also demonstrated to her subordinates that she had a real interest in and understanding of their work.

Coaching Improves Performance and Job Satisfaction

At the end of the year's coaching, this executive's boss summarized: "I see [her] growth happening right before my own eyes, and it is excellent."

Moreover, the executive herself reflected, "Through my relationship with a coach, I now see things differently. I feel more valued by the company since they invested in me as someone they wanted to develop and keep in the company. [My boss] was the champion to ensure that I received all feedback possible."

Specifically, the executive increased her satisfaction level in working with difficult people. She was better able to deal with them to get the job done and did not feel she had to hide from them.

By working with a coach, she received validation of her judgment of subordinates. This gave her confidence to deal with difficult personnel on a daily basis and increased her confidence in personnel decisions. And, while she was not accustomed to asking others' opinions before she acted, she became more aware of asking others and sharing information rather than being dogmatic in her approach.

Conclusion

Executive coaching is not a "one size fits all" exercise. Each executive who participates in a coaching relationship will learn different lessons, based on that executive's own performance and own needs. What is most important is that the executive be open to feedback and willing to listen to others' perceptions and ideas. Good leaders do just that. The belief that the manager must have all the answers is a huge fallacy that limits the success of executives and prevents them from learning the lessons that come with time and experience.

Barbara Pate Glacel, *Ph.D., is principal of The Glacel Group of Virginia and Brussels, Belgium. She is author of a business bestseller on teams. She works with individuals, teams, and organizations in the Fortune 500 and not-for-profit arenas. She has over thirty years' experience in executive coaching and leadership development at all levels of organizations. She is a well-known author and public speaker and has consulted in Europe, Asia, and South Africa.*

Collaborative Management

Peter R. Garber

Summary

Collaborative management is a new term to describe a work environment in which a variety of people review decisions to ensure that a diversity of viewpoints is considered before a final decision is reached. Collaborative management most likely exists in a work environment based on mutual trust and cooperation. It is not a cure for interpersonal problems between employees but more likely exists as a conscious effort to move forward to a different level of working relationships. In other words, you need to learn to work together in a cooperative manner before you can expect to be able to create a collaborative environment.

What Is Collaborative Management?

Webster's dictionary defines collaborate as *to work jointly with others or together, especially in an intellectual endeavor.* Collaborate comes from Latin meaning *to labor together.*

Collaborative management is a term to describe what might be considered an ideal work environment in which everyone is dedicated to achieving a common objective. Collaboration is the engine of teamwork. Collaboration is an attitude that everyone must share in order for it to work. When collaboration becomes a guiding force and an operating principle in an organization, the whole working environment begins to shift. Decisions are based on collective experiences and knowledge. There is more ownership concerning decisions, less finger pointing, and the blame game disappears. Collaborative decisions typically are less risky, as different perspectives and expertise are brought into the decision-making process proactively rather than reactively.

Like most management concepts, collaborative management is not easily defined. It is a state of mind or an attitude. Nor is a collaborative management work environment easily achieved or maintained. There are any number of obstacles or variables that could impede the development of collaborative management in an organization. Obviously, collaborative management cannot exist in a workplace in which employees are preoccupied with mistrust, doubt, infighting, insecurity, and so on.

Description of the Collaborative Management Model

Figure 1 depicts the hierarchy of interpersonal relationships that should exist to support collaborative management.

Trust

The foundation of any collaborative relationship must be built on mutual trust. Collaborative management requires that everyone involved in the process trust everyone else. If this trust does not exist, it will be virtually impossible to create a collaborative management process in the organization.

Cooperation

Collaboration requires cooperation among the participants. Everyone must cooperate with everyone else to make the process work effectively. If a key stakeholder in the

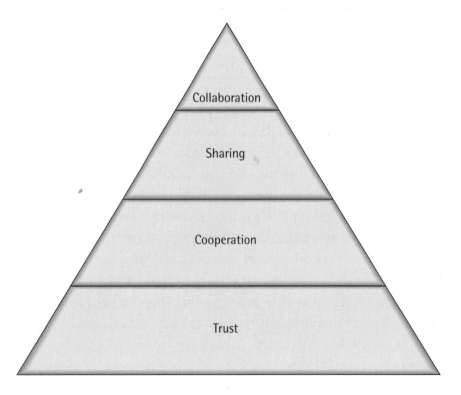

Figure 1.   The Hierarchy of Relationships That Support Collaborative Management

process doesn't cooperate with the others in the collaborative process, the entire effort will fail for everyone.

Sharing

Collaboration involves sharing information, confidences, thoughts, feelings, and so on. Everyone must share for the collaborative process to proceed. If stakeholders begin to hold back information, the entire collaborative process can be negatively affected—and even stopped.

Collaboration

Trust, cooperation, and sharing lead to collaboration. Collaboration is a progressive process in which each step must be achieved in order to move to the next level.

Collaborative management is that state in which the decisions, actions, directions, and visions of an organization are determined with key stakeholders in the process involved. It is typically agreed (albeit usually silently) among co-workers that each individual will consult with the other stakeholders before moving forward concerning matters of common interest and consequence. In a collaborative management work environment, consultations and discussions are the norm before action. Although not as efficient as single-opinioned decisions, any inefficiency created by collaborative decisions typically is recovered by the absence of problems encountered as a result of this process. Redundancy in decision making is not necessarily a bad thing when it prevents much larger problems later on.

Advantages of Collaborative Management

Collaborative management works best when different functions are involved. Each area brings a new perspective, often one not fully appreciated by the others. As a result, the interests of each area are better represented and served by decisions made in an organization. There is also more ownership of the final decision and less criticism from others who are not included in the process. Often, contrary opinions are because someone was left out of the decision-making process, rather than that he or she disagrees with the decision itself.

Collaborative consensus is created when those consulted all agree on a course of action or a decision. Consensus in this case means that everyone in the decision-making loop agrees to move forward with a certain agreed-on action, regardless of whether it was their first choice or not. This results in collaborative agreements that immediately are *owned* by those involved and vested in the process.

Potential Pitfalls

However, there may also be a downside to collaboration. An organization may experience a number of syndromes that are counterproductive. Perhaps the most common of these pitfalls is what could be termed *collaborative conservatism,* in that groups have a tendency to err on the conservative side. As the collaborative process proceeds, a conservative viewpoint will inevitably be presented and considered. Groups tend to gravitate toward "safe" decisions. Caution must be employed to ensure that a collaborative management system doesn't play so safe that it avoids any type of risk. Risks do need to be taken, and collaboration can be an excellent testing ground for being sure the right decisions are made at the right times. On the other hand, a group may take too great a risk, believing itself insulated from accountability—a variation of the idea of safety in numbers. Either extreme is problematic and should be monitored by the organization as a whole.

Another risk in collaborative management systems is the group adapting the opinion of a single strong voice. In this case, you have only the illusion of collaborative consensus. There may also be factions within the group that take control of the collaborative process, omitting other members' views. The collaborative consortiums can distort the validity of the collaborative process and pose a danger to the entire organization if not recognized and challenged.

A collaborative management process may require a cultural change in your organization. Collaboration must be *expected* to happen. It doesn't have to begin with great fanfare or pageantry. It can begin subtly and discretely. The only people who really need to know that it has been implemented are those directly involved. However, it won't take long before others realize a change has taken place. At first there may be some pushback as a collaborative decision-making process takes more time. Expect to hear some criticisms, such as that you are getting more bureaucratic and less efficient. This may be true, at least at first. But others will begin to see the benefits of collaborative management. Once decisions are made, there is less bureaucracy and red tape. As a collaborative process becomes more comfortable for everyone involved, the decision-making process can move ahead with all stakeholders involved from the onset. As you learn more about how others feel on certain issues, their positions can be represented, even in their absence. The decisions will begin to be made with greater consensus. The true power of collaboration can be realized and problems mitigated earlier. Others, even those outside of the decision-making loop, will become knowledgeable about how decisions are made and will know what to expect. They may even learn to anticipate different decisions based on the uniformity and consistency that collaborative management decisions can create.

Rewarding Collaboration

Collaborative thinking can become the norm in a work environment that nurtures such a management system. People can learn to think collaboratively, although it is counter-intuitive. Our work systems often reward individualism and performance instead. Employees may feel that their personal contributions are obscured by a group effort. If an organization wishes to establish a system of collaborative management, it must recognize this tendency and reinforce people for contributing to group efforts. The old adage that two heads are better than one must be the cornerstone of any collaborative management operating system.

Seven Steps to Establishing Collaborative Management

1. Review Your Decision-Making Process

First understand how key decisions are currently being made in your organization and decide how comfortable you are with the current process. You may already have a collaborative decision-making process in place and not be fully aware that it exists.

2. Determine Whether Collaborative Management Is Right for Your Organization

Collaborative management may not be right for your organization if the culture, norms, expectations, and style are not supportive of or conducive to this approach. Trying to fight these forces may ultimately be less productive than trying to improve on the type of management and decision-making style that currently exists.

3. Decide Who the Stakeholders Are

Once you have determined that collaborative management could be beneficial to your organization, identify who should be included in the process. Getting the right stakeholders involved is critical to success.

4. Establish Parameters

Even collaboration has to have boundaries and rules. Make clear the scope of authority those involved in collaborative management have and what limitations exist. Determining these parameters up-front will prevent misunderstanding later on.

5. Help Decision Makers Understand Their Roles

An extension of these parameters is everyone understanding the role he or she plays in the process. If there are certain decisions (usually connected with one's position in the organization) that individuals are expected to make, these must be clearly defined. Collaborative management doesn't mean that you no longer rely on the expertise of individuals to influence decisions when appropriate. However, these decisions should be discussed and reviewed by others with diverse perspectives.

6. Monitor the Process

Monitor the process on a regular basis (particularly in the beginning stages of implementation) to ensure that collaboration is truly occurring. Be mindful of some of the pitfalls described earlier.

7. Recognize and Reward Collaborative Management

It is very important that you recognize and reward collaboration if you want it to continue and thrive in your organization. Review your reinforcement systems to ensure that your rewards are not counter to supporting a collaborative management system.

Peter R. Garber *is currently manager of Equal Employment Opportunity at PPG Industries, Inc., in Pittsburgh, Pennsylvania. He is author of seven books on a variety of business topics, including his most recent work,* Giving and Receiving Performance Feedback. *He is also a training specialist and consultant. Mr. Garber is a regular contributor of activities and learning instruments to the* Annuals.

Results of the Effective Change Survey

Rick Maurer

Summary

This article shows the results of an Effective Change Survey we conducted across organizations. The results confirmed our assumption that four major areas are critical to the success of major changes in organizations. As predicted, there was an inverse correlation between low scores and high failure rates. In other words, when these areas were ignored, the likelihood of failure increased. But we were surprised to learn how critically important the first of those areas—making a compelling case for change—was in contributing to the overall success of a new initiative.

What's the difference between those changes in organizations that get results and those that don't? We knew that only about one-third of all major changes succeeded. But we wanted to know why. What sets apart the successful changes? What could we learn from those who do it well?

So we conducted an Effective Change Survey. Close to two hundred and fifty people responded. They told us about major changes in their organizations, ranging from mergers to new software systems to reorganizations. The responses came from a range of types and sizes of organizations, although many were from large organizations. Most of the projects they described were budgeted between $100K and a few million dollars. People could rate the change on a 1 to 5 scale, from "a stunning success" down to "made matters significantly worse." (The details of the survey can be found on the last page of this article.)

We based the survey on our assumption that four things had to be addressed during a major change:

1. Recognizing that *making a strong case for change* was a critical component.

2. Leaders kicked off the change (*get started*) by involving people and setting a clear vision.

3. Leaders took certain actions and put systems in place that would help *sustain commitment* to the change over the long term.

4. When problems did occur, the leaders of the change used effective methods to *get back on track*.

We wanted to see whether the data supported our own experience with clients. Our assumptions proved to be correct. These four areas seem to be of fundamental importance to those leading major changes.

Making a Case

The most important element was the ability to make a compelling case for change. In 96 percent of the changes rated as "stunning successes," *many* stakeholders saw a compelling need for the change. (And in 73 percent of those highly successful changes, *most* stakeholders saw a compelling need.) Stakeholders understood:

- Current financial situation of the organization;

- Economic or market forces facing the organization;

- Economic or market forces facing their industry;

- Why this change was critical; and

- How the challenges facing the organization would affect them directly.

There was a direct link between making a case and success. The fewer who saw a need for a change, the greater the failure rate. In 22 percent of those changes that "made matters significantly worse," only some stakeholders saw a need for a change. And in 65 percent of those failed changes, people thought it was a waste of time and money.

The organizations that did make a strong case for change did well in all of the other categories: getting started, sustaining commitment, and getting back on track. This suggests that they take change management seriously and attend to all aspects of the change, from planning through to completion. They never seem to drop the ball.

There was one significant missed opportunity. Even in the organizations where most saw a compelling need for a change, only 31 percent answered, "the overall culture was such that most people generally understood the challenges and opportunities facing them" (61 percent answered "somewhat"). According to James Collins (2002), organizations that create a culture in which people understand the business challenges seldom need to worry about getting alignment, motivation, or even managing change. While there is more to success than just making a case, when people do "get it," less time is wasted getting ready for each new initiative.

Getting Started

Those leading successful changes addressed each of the following:

- Almost all stakeholders were represented in the planning process;

- Everybody was kept informed as plans developed;

- Various points of view were encouraged;

- A clear vision (outcome) was created;

- Sound tactical plans were developed; and

- Timelines and measures of success were created.

Clear vision topped the list. In 73 percent of the "stunning successes," there was a clear vision created for this initiative. In poorly run changes, those in which the organization was "significantly worse off," a clear vision was in place 11 percent of the time. The bulleted items listed above were usually absent in changes that failed.

We were surprised by the lack of importance leaders placed on developing contingency plans during the getting started phase. Only 28 percent of the organizations with successful changes developed contingency plans. We expected that score to be much higher.

Sustaining Commitment

Sustaining commitment to a major change is difficult. It often takes months, even years, to get from planning to results. During that time, priorities can shift, attention may drift, and leadership can change. In the successful changes, we found that each of the following was in place throughout the life of the project:

- Strong leadership;

- Everyone understood his/her role in the change;

- Sufficient resources were made available to support planning and implementation;

- Clear metrics (measures of success) were used throughout;

- People felt ownership in the process;

- People felt ownership in the outcome; and

- People were recognized for meeting goals at every major milestone.

In those changes that "made matters significantly worse," *0 percent* attended to any of those items to a "significant degree." Most scored all items low, except for strong leadership. Thirty-three percent rated it "not at all"; 11 percent gave it a "2"; 33 percent said "somewhat"; and 22 percent gave it a "4." And, as mentioned, zero scored it a "5."

Getting Back on Track

Of those who rated their changes a "stunning success," 44 percent said that they didn't need to worry about getting things back on track. This suggests that, by attending to the other three areas, the likelihood of problems—especially resistance to change—decreases significantly.

However, in those instances for which leaders involved in successful changes did need to attend to the threat of the initiative derailing, a high percentage said that they:

- Brought people together to explore the real reasons why the change was faltering;

- Listened to people who were resisting and tried to incorporate their concerns;

- Treated those who opposed this change with respect; and

- Used contingency plans developed during the planning stages.

We were surprised that only 8 percent of the leaders were willing to admit that their actions (or perhaps their reputation) was having a negative impact on this change. (Although in the most extreme failures, none of the leaders admitted mistakes.)

Leaders of failed changes consistently neglected to attend to the bulleted items listed above.

Putting the Survey to Work

There is a big gap between what leaders *know* and what they actually *do.* In our work with clients, we find that a majority of executives and managers know what it takes to lead change successfully. They often speak eloquently about ways to make a case, get started, sustain commitment, and get things back on track. In other words, we believe that many people leading changes in organizations would agree that the items listed in this survey need to be in place.

However, something gets in the way of putting that knowledge into practice. It's as if people disregard their own wisdom. Perhaps it is time pressure or a belief that there is always a better—and faster—way to do things. We believe that having a way to think about change—a theory of change, if you will—can help leaders attend to those things that are most likely to lead to success. We invite you to use the four steps that we use with our own clients—make a case for change, get started, sustain commitment, and get back on track—as a way to focus attention on the critical human part of major change.

About the Survey

Two hundred forty-five people responded to this survey. They came from both large and small organizations with 37 percent of people reporting on changes that took place in large organizations. The types of changes ranged from reorganizations (24 percent) to mergers (12 percent) to major new software systems (15 percent). Roles of those who responded included the following: consultants (27 percent); managers in charge of some aspect of the change (19 percent); employees involved with the change (19 percent); and leaders (26 percent). Thirty-two percent of the changes were budgeted at over $1 million, and 18 percent over $100K.

Reference

Collins, J. (2002). *Good to great.* New York: HarperBusiness.

Rick Maurer *is author of the* Change Without Migraines™ *series of books on leading change. He is an advisor on change to a broad range of clients in different industries, including aerospace, healthcare, chemical manufacturing, and government. He has written several other books on change, including* Beyond the Wall of Resistance *and* Why Don't You Want What I Want?

Teams of a New Generation
Defining the 21st Century Experiential Training Agenda

Greg Robinson and Mark Rose

Summary

Times have changed, and those changes have exposed the weakness of old paradigms. Sustainable success will require that people inside organizations become adept at learning and changing in response to a dynamic environment. To do otherwise will certainly mean difficulty, if not demise. The implications for organizations and the consultants who work with them are many. Not the least of these is the ability to develop a workforce capable of excelling with the demands of the emerging world. Experiential educators can have a significant contribution to make if they understand the true developmental requirements of the age. This article has a three-fold purpose: (1) provide a description of the emerging demands of the 21st Century team; (2) identify critical thinking "meta-skills" that will equip team members to excel in a collaborative environment; and (3) describe how the experiential educator can begin to assert an effective influence on the workforce.

The Emerging Demands on the 21st Century Team

There was a time when teams were made up of individuals carrying out assigned tasks together. In these teams, the members worked in close proximity to one another because their basic shared work involved some kind of raw material. The interdependence of the team members was observable and tangible. The action of one person had immediate and concrete consequences for others. Since the work was already defined, efficiency was of the utmost importance. Consequently, stability or a lack of variance was critical. Such teams generally came from one part of the organization, with one senior leader providing one set of expectations. The team was held together through a set of rules, procedures, and codes defined by the single voice of authority.

In today's world, the majority of teams are called to work under very different circumstances with very different priorities and outcomes. In today's workplace, many teams do not work in close proximity to one another. They come from many different parts of the company, or even the world, as they gather to develop a vision of their work and a solution to their challenges. Consequently, the interdependence of these teams is less tangible and observable. This is due to the fact that the raw material of much of the team's work is information or knowledge. Rarely are teams assigned to a single, defined task, but rather are challenged to solve complex problems with many different tasks, using many different specialties from many different parts of the organization. This results in multiple voices of authority providing their own sets of expectations, priorities, and values. New generation teams are held together by a shared vision of a desired end result and principles and values that determine how the team should pursue that shared vision.

In the end, not only has the workplace changed, but the very nature of teamwork itself has changed. No longer do teams work in a stable environment with defined work. Most often they work in a rapidly changing environment in which the work must first be defined and then carried out. In addition, teams do not have long-term life spans. As more and more organizations move toward project-based work, workers will belong to multiple teams or change teams frequently.

The demands placed on teams and the individuals who make up those teams have changed. These demands now include forming quickly, accessing the collective intelligence, maintaining flexibility, and facilitating their own development. The underlying capability enabling the successful team today is learning. This type of learning creates awareness of personal assumptions and challenges mental models. It equips team members to be flexible and appropriately innovative because of the purposeful use of differences and an ever-broadening perspective (Robinson & Rose, 2004). In order to be capable of such learning, individuals and teams must be able to step back from their roles, their actions, their experiences, and their relationships in order to understand the cause of certain events and actions. Only by understanding why and how events or actions came to be can teams learn from their experience and thus replicate success or eliminate mistakes. Ultimately, this is not just a matter of technique or process. This requires a deeper level of development. The following are some of the critical development tasks that are a part of the 21st Century learning agenda.

Critical Developmental Tasks

Separate Self from Others

The first development task is to *separate self from others*. Many times people are so intertwined with other people that they cannot step back from the relationships and determine on their own what they should do. They are convinced that their own progress or success is dependent on someone else changing or doing something. Systems thinking helps us understand that, although there is interdependence, my real power is in changing myself rather than focusing on others. I must be able to see myself outside of a relationship so that I can determine my own actions. As long as I believe that someone else must change in order for me to succeed or grow, I am stuck trying to change someone I do not have the power to change in the first place.

Experiential programming is uniquely designed to develop this capability within team members because of the use of experiential learning activities (structured experiences). Structured experiences accelerate the manifestation of team dynamics, but do so in a limited container of time and context so that those dynamics can be reflected on.

Example

I use an activity I call Yurt Rope to teach this principle to teams. In the activity, the entire group steps inside a large rope circle. Group members place the rope on their lower backs just above their hips. Everyone then leans back on the rope until the team is balanced against the tension in the rope. I start with some observations about systems as a set of interdependent relationships where a change in one place influences the whole system. I shift my weight and watch the entire group react to regain its balance. After some more discussion, I offer a task that will teach the main point of this exercise. As I am leaning on the rope, I tell the group to make me stand up straight. Nearly every time, members' first response is to start pulling hard on the rope, trying to make me stand up. The more they pull, the more I lean back and resist. After a few moments of this tug-o-war, they realize they are not getting anywhere. At some point, someone speaks up and suggests that they just let go of the rope. They muse, "If there is no pressure on the rope, he will either stand up or fall down."

Now they have an awakening. As long as they focus on trying to change me, they are continually frustrated by my resistance. However, when they separate themselves from me and focus on themselves, they realize that by changing themselves they can influence me. Their real power is to define and change themselves, rather than trying to change me.

Separate Self from Experience

The second developmental task is to *separate self from experience.* Too many people see their experiences as a series of events and tend to look for simplistic relationships between things. People who see the world this way tend not to understand their contribution to what is happening. Critical reflection teaches people to step back and view their experiences as a whole. By doing so, they will be able see the connection of things across time and they will be able to see their own contribution to the situation. They have experiences; experiences do not have them. The significant result of this capability is that individuals realize how they contribute to the outcomes they are experiencing with the team. When I recognize my patterns of behavior, I become free to ask the question, "What can I do differently than what I always do to affect a different outcome?"

Example

I was working with a corporate group on a low element ropes course circuit. The circuit was made up of eleven elements fashioned with an outer ring and several elements that crisscrossed the center. In the very center was a teeter-totter platform. The team was struggling a good deal trying to get the platform balanced and keep it balanced. After several minutes, I noticed one of the members step off of the platform and sit down on the side. Seeing this as a potential opening, I went over and asked him how he thought they were doing. "This is the way it always is," he said. I responded, "How so?" "They will keep going at each other until everyone is exhausted and then they will be ready to listen." I asked him, "Is this what you tend to do?" He answered, "Yes, I sit on the side and wait them out." Now came the learning opportunity. This gentleman was convinced that he could not make progress because of other people. He was stuck in a role that the system required him to play. Since he could not change the team, he was powerless to change anything. I left him with a question, "I wonder, is there anything you could do that is different from what you always do that could influence a different outcome?" I then left and moved to the other side of the area. In just a few moments, he got up, walked over, stepped on the platform, went to the far end, leaned against a tree and balanced the platform. The team immediately turned its attention to the remainder of the project and completed it in very good time. This participant had learned to separate himself from his experience. He could see that his pattern of behavior contributed to the pattern of the team as much as did the pattern of any vocal member of the team. Most importantly, he realized that he could take action and influence a different outcome.

Separate Thinking from Feeling

The final developmental task is to *separate thinking from feeling*. All of our actions are influenced by what we think, our mental models and assumptions, as well as by what we are feeling. Too often, we do not pay attention to what is going on inside of us. The result is that we often are reactive in our actions rather than intentional. Another way of thinking about this is that, when I become anxious, I take actions that I may say are trying to help the situation, but in reality they are an attempt to relieve my anxiety. The outcome is that my actions are automated, knee-jerk responses that tend to be my least effective and least creative responses to the situation.

In teams, the result is that, the more individuals react to their anxiety, the more anxiety the team shares collectively. This limits the team's ability to see its situation from new and creative perspectives that could introduce team members to a more effective solution. It also leads to team members who continually rescue others who are in difficult circumstances, rather than support the member in trouble as a solution is discovered. This can lead to a level of dependence and immaturity among the team members.

Example

My favorite method of teaching this capability is to use a climbing wall. As the climber begins to make his or her way up the wall, invariably there comes a point at which he or she needs some assistance in determining the path to the top. The climber is too close, too tied up in the task, to see the big picture. The team can step back and help the climber determine the path to take. However, often this is not the case. Rather than describing the big picture, with all the possible routes and the choices available to the climber, the team begins to yell out orders: "Put your foot there." "Move your hand to the right." The more the climber struggles, the louder and more intense the commands are shouted.

In an attempt to help the climber, the team is in actuality doing the opposite of what it intends. The more team members press the climber and the louder their communication becomes, the more anxious the climber becomes. The more the climber struggles, the more anxious the team gets, resulting in more reactive behavior. What the team members do not realize is that how they are choosing to help is more a reaction to their own discomfort in watching a teammate struggle than an honest attempt to help the climber. In order to really be helpful, team members must recognize the emotion within them, step back from it, and act in a purposeful way—focused on helping the climber succeed. If the team can do so, members will not only help the climber complete the climb, but they will help the climber reason through the best way to climb in the future. The knowledge transfer back to the workplace is that, by supporting a struggling teammate and helping him or her gain clarity through good questions, that teammate will not only work through the current issue, but will learn to be more effective in the long run.

Conclusion

The demands of today's workplace require us to define our own identities. This definition requires a higher level of cognitive complexity. The ability to step outside of ourselves, our experiences, and our relationships will allow us to see them more clearly. As our clarity grows, we can intentionally choose actions that will be purposeful and effective rather than reactive and defensive. Experiential programming is uniquely situated to help with this development. Facilitators must realize that they can have a greater long-term influence by using their activities and processing to teach teams to see their own dynamics. Ropes courses, indoor initiatives, and even the real-world experiences of work are learning labs to develop maturity and advanced capabilities.

Reference

Robinson, G., & Rose, M. (2004). *A leadership paradox: Influencing others by defining yourself.* Bloomington, IN: Authorhouse.

Greg Robinson *is currently president of Challenge Quest, LLC, in Pryor, Oklahoma. Dr. Robinson has a Ph.D. in organizational behavior and leadership from The Union Institute and University in Cincinnati, Ohio. His professional career has concentrated in the areas of team development, leadership development, facilitation, and consulting with organizational change efforts. He is the author of* Teams for a New Generation: An Introduction to Collective Learning.

Mark Rose *is a training coordinator for Enogex, a natural gas processing company. His main focus is equipping teams with skills and tools to become more effective. He received his master's of human relations degree from The University of Oklahoma. He has worked as co-facilitator in a series of training videos,* Trainer Games in Action: Volume One and Two, *which show how trainers can use activities to help learners retain information.*

A Coaching Challenge
Surviving the Arrogant Boss
H.B. Karp

Summary

In endeavoring to help executives and managers achieve higher levels of effectiveness, coaches may find themselves dealing with a number of factors. One of the most challenging can be working with a manager whose direct superior suffers from an overabundance of self-importance, also known as hubris. This article presents some background on the concept of hubris, points out several telltale signs that hubris may be an issue, and provides some suggestions for how coaches and managers can best deal with a hubristic leader.

Historically, OD practitioners who coach managers and executives are concerned with developing skills that increase the effectiveness of that manager or executive. Regardless of the nature of the organization, the generic objectives of the coach are twofold:

1. To develop the manager's awareness of the barriers to accomplishing the vision and goals (results desired) of the organization; and

2. To develop the manager's people skills that are necessary to promote stronger and more capable individual and team efforts to accomplish those goals.

Proficient coaches easily recognize the more common barriers, such as poor planning and forecasting, inadequate budgeting and financing, scarce resources, and inadequate people skills, to name but a few. In terms of "poor people skills," lack of awareness, incorrect assumptions about human behavior, and poor listening skills contribute to this phenomenon.

This work is dedicated to Paul Trible, former U.S. Senator and the current president of Christopher Newport University in Newport News, Virginia.

Today there is a more deadly and a much-more-difficult-to-recognize concern for OD coaches embedded in the cultures of both the public and the private sectors. This is the phenomenon of *hubris,* which is a particularly toxic and virulent form of arrogance. Hubris has been traditionally associated with military and political leaders, but is just as prevalent in today's organizational settings. Just a few examples include people like Tyco's Dennis Kozlowski, Enron's Kenneth Lay, Martha Stewart's Martha Stewart, and HealthSouth's Richard Scrushy, who went so far as to have bronze statues of himself erected on the grounds of corporate headquarters.

The objective and the challenge of this article is to foster an awareness and a concern about the nature and the prevalence of this devastating dynamic and to begin dialogue on how to develop coaching methods to impart the necessary "survival skills" to managers who have to maintain their effectiveness while working for a hubristic boss.

Definitions and a Little History

The *Random House Dictionary* (1967, p. 690) defines hubris simply as *excessive pride; arrogance.* In looking more closely at that definition, we could note that *excessive pride* is dysfunctional only by its definition, that it is "excessive." As for *arrogance,* a case can even be made for that, when defined as "supreme confidence in one's self-worth" (Karp, 1985, p. 185). In the realm of organizational behavior and interpersonal relationships, however, hubris is far more complex than either of these defining terms. A more comprehensive operational definition for hubris is needed, and I would like to suggest the following: *"Hubris is a deepening sense of well-being and pride that grows into a delusion of unassailability and total control over one's environment"* (Karp & Jackson, 2003).

Hubris has been around for as long we have been living and working within groups. The word "hubris" itself originates in Greek mythology and refers to the self-image of humans who attempt to take on godlike attributes. It goes as far back, if not farther, as the biblical interdiction, *"Pride goeth before destruction and a haughty spirit before a fall"* (Proverbs xvi: 18).

One of the most well-known, historical acknowledgments of hubris is apparent in ancient Rome. When a victorious general was accorded a triumph, he would lead his army through the streets of Rome to the frenetic accolades of the citizenry. The general who was being so honored rode in the lead chariot with a slave standing behind him holding a laurel wreath over his head. The slave also had the responsibility of constantly repeating the phrase, "Remember that thou art only a man." Historic political examples of the destructive nature of hubris are Julius Caesar, Napoleon Bonaparte, and Adolph Hitler. More modern examples include the evangelist Jim Bakker and Walt Disney's

Michael Eisner. All of these people were well on their way to achieving all they dreamed of until they crossed the line.

Attributes of Hubris

The attributes that metamorphose into hubris are absolutely essential for human effectiveness. Some of these include self-confidence, pride in accomplishment, and self-esteem. However, when these attributes become overriding, they begin to mutate into hubris.

Hubris is a *quantitative* condition and operates much like any other quantitative attribute. To illustrate with a physical example, good health requires a body temperature of something around 98.6 degrees. When the body becomes ill, the temperature increases and, as it rises, a temperature becomes a "fever." Hubris operates the same way psychologically. As self-confidence increases, a healthy threshold is eventually reached. If, however, the self-confidence increases past this threshold, hubris begins to emerge and takes on an increasingly firmer grip on one's perceptions. If left unchecked, it eventually evolves into a highly toxic form of self-delusion. Hubris is a classic example of way too much of a good thing.

The above metaphor breaks down only in one place. With temperature, the worse it becomes the worse you feel; with hubris, it's just the opposite, that is, the worse it gets, the *better* you feel. One of the most devastating aspects of hubris is that the more convinced leaders become of their own ability to prevail under the worst of circumstances and to be invulnerable in the process, the higher the probability that they sooner or later will "crash and burn."

The Fate of Those Who Follow

When hubris is discussed, it is invariably done with respect to individuals who have been infected. The reality is, however, that while the hubristic administrator can be said to be experiencing "a suffering good time," the same cannot be said for those who are doomed to serve below such an individual in the organization. For those who have to live with the effects of the decisions coming from a hubristic administrator, it is almost invariably a case of just plain suffering.

This was certainly the case at the university where I worked some years prior to accepting my current position. When I joined that institution, it was a decent and efficient place to work: people were mutually supportive throughout the system, and organizational members seemed to be treated with respect by the president and his administration. The president appeared to be genuinely concerned about issues that affected the faculty and student body; he was very approachable and he always seemed to have a good word. Over time, however, the organization slowly but steadily changed. Image became increasingly more important than function; major changes in curricula and priorities occurred that did not seem to make sense to anyone outside of the central administration; and the institution began to look more and more like the institution from which the president himself had graduated. It appeared that a monument was in the process of being erected.

Previously supportive administrators became micro-managers or were removed and replaced by those who were willing to micro-manage. The first obligation of new administrative hires and those who were promoted was to push the "party line," as handed down by the president; any overt statement of disagreement with the new policies was punished, and a special room for reprimanding lower administrators who appeared to be non-supportive of the president's policies was implemented and became legendary. Morale was slowly strangled, energy was diverted into self-protection, caution began to replace creativity and excitement, younger qualified people started looking for opportunities in other institutions, and, as of this writing, the entire system continues to be modified and reshaped to accommodate one man's vision of glorifying himself. Clearly the message here is that hubris is not only toxic to the person who has it, but can be equally damaging to others in the environment and to the organization itself.

No CEO, executive, or manager starts out hubristic; nor is every one destined to end up this way. If and when it occurs, the process is cumulative and progresses at varying rates, depending on the individual. What does appear to occur is that, regardless of how slowly or quickly it takes hold, the process accelerates over time. That is, it might take some time for you to notice the first symptoms, particularly if you happen to be more than one level below the afflicted administrator in the hierarchy; but once the symptoms appear, they increase at a more rapid and obvious rate.

The View from Below

It is reasonable to assume that, in many cases, at least part of the problem that your client is facing is the hubristic style of his or her superior. As a coach, it is important to be aware of the signs yourself so you can work with this factor if it is impinging at all on your client's effectiveness. Some indicators that the process might be starting, or is well underway—depending on how far down the system your client "lives"—are Enforced Versus Shared Vision; An Open Door Is Closed; The First-Person Complex; Reflected Glory;

Noblesse Oblige; Transferable Grandeur; and Self-Image: The New Organizational Objective.

1. Enforced Vision vs. Shared Vision

Visionary leadership has come to be recognized as the hallmark of the truly effective executive. The term implies that all who are visionary share their vision for the organization. This provides goal orientation, role clarification, and a common interpersonal bond, regardless of where one is in the system. Bateman and Snell (2002, p. 380) quote several executives who make the point: Robert Swiggert, former chair of Kollmorgen Corporation, states, "The leader's job is to create a vision." Mark Leslie, a successful entrepreneur, maintains, "If there is no vision, there is no business"; and Joe Niven, an MIS director, states that leaders are "painters of the vision and architects of the journey." These few quotes are representative of the importance that creating and maintaining the vision has in today's organization. As in every pirate movie I saw as a kid, every treasure map had a big "X" drawn on it, and only the captain had access to the map and knew how to get there. His main job was to inspire the crew and keep them moving in the right direction.

Sharing the vision is essential; *inflicting* the vision, on the other hand, becomes increasingly counterproductive. You can usually tell this is happening when any questioning of the vision is looked on as a threat or "blasphemy." Transitioning from "sharing" to "inflicting" can be very subtle. It slowly moves from participating in a commonly held ideal for the organization to blindly following the self-serving goals of the leader's ego needs, still phrased in organizational terms.

2. An Open Door Is Closed

Many of the more effective leaders are recognized by their obvious "people skills." While effective in meeting or exceeding their task objectives in terms of results, they also are adept at bringing to the surface all the energy and commitment their direct reports bring to the work setting each day. Such executives tend to be outgoing, supportive, tolerant of reasonable mistakes (often seeing them as an opportunity for growth), safe to be around, and able to build and maintain a team spirit. Quite frequently, they maintain an "open door policy," that is, welcoming subordinates to share their ideas and concerns, safely, at their own pace.

However, *role locking* can frequently occur in this kind of administrator, who is quick to win the approbation and loyalty from those whom he or she leads. Role-lock is a condition whereby the administrator is using *only* the leadership style that gets reinforced by the direct reports. The longer the administrator leads in this highly popular style, the more consistently those below in the organization reinforce it. Other situationally effective leadership styles begin to fade so that, eventually, the only leadership style available to the administrator is the one that everybody loves, which, in turn, continues to be positively reinforced. This constant positive reinforcement, in turn, leads to the inevitable onset of hubris. As hubris begins to increase, the leader's availability begins to decrease at approximately the same rate.

What began as, "Feel free to drop by any time" slowly, inevitably, turns into, "You are hereby summoned to appear." The administrator is no longer seen by the coffee pot, in the lunch facility, or at social gatherings unless he or she sponsors it as a formal obligation. The administrator's office slowly transitions into a "throne room." Time with the administrator is now looked on as a "privilege" to those deemed lucky enough to be granted an audience in the *Presence.*

3. The First Person Complex

The hubristic leader begins to think of the organization in the first person and him- or herself in the third. Cleopatra's famous quote, "I am Egypt" or DeGaulle's declaration, "I am France" lets you know that the pinnacle of hubris has finally been attained. Of course, nobody in his or her right mind today runs around saying, "I am Amalgamated Widgets" or "I am Joe's Bar & Grill"; however, it can be seen happening just below the surface.

One of the characteristics that defines the effective human being is the person's ability to maintain strong and clear boundaries—between the self and others and between the self and the environment. The same holds true for the effective organizational leader. As hubris becomes stronger, boundary awareness between the leader and the organization becomes weaker and, occasionally, even manifests itself in the form of the leader beginning to refer to himself or herself in the third person, that is, they refer to themselves by name, rather than using the pronoun "I" when making a point.

4. Basking in the Reflected Glory

Hubristic leaders have a unique vision of themselves and may begin to look for "other" celebrities who can appreciate them. Certainly there have been national leaders who have been frequently seen with luminaries from the entertainment and sports worlds. President Kennedy was one such leader and was considered by some to be an honorary member of the "Rat Pack" headed up by Frank Sinatra and that also included President Kennedy's brother-in-law, the actor Peter Lawford, as an active member. To President Kennedy's credit, he immediately broke all implied association with this group after the disastrous Bay of Pigs invasion.

Certainly, making and maintaining good contacts with prestigious members of the community is the job of any CEO or high-status opinion maker. As with all things pertaining to hubris, the question is how much of it is helpful and how appropriate the contacts are. There is no formula that I can offer you to help make such determinations except for the observation that if the contact and exposure do more to aggrandize the leader than they do to reflect well on the best parts of the organization, the leader is operating out of hubris. If I were to give advice, it would be to be slow to judge, but trust your gut.

5. Noblesse Oblige

To maintain hubris, one has to be constantly and positively reinforced. This can't be accomplished unless there is a venue for the approbation to occur. The objective of the hubristic leader here is not to make contact with subordinates, but rather to make an *appearance.* The leader makes a showing at the company picnic or Christmas party for a brief period of time, and everybody says, "Gee, what a wonderful guy." This is quite different from the CEO showing up at the picnic when it starts, lending a hand in setting up, and spending the afternoon talking with people, drinking beer, and playing softball as a way of *authentically* interacting.

Lee Iaccoca, in my opinion, turned out to be one of the most successful CEOs in the country when he took over Chrysler. The story goes that one of the ways he had of rewarding outstanding work from first-line supervisors was to invite that supervisor to have lunch with him in the "Power Tower."

Iaccoca not only enjoyed the blessed feeling of "noblesse oblige," he could bask in the awe of the supervisor who was so privileged to be afforded this all-too-brief, but glorious, elevation. My guess is that, while some supervisors may have felt really honored, most felt either terribly patronized or incredibly uncomfortable. What might have worked better would have been for Iaccoca to meet the supervisor at the supervisor's favorite restaurant or grille and have lunch there . . . if spending time with the supervisor was what it was all about.

6. Transferable Grandeur

One rare but not unknown variation of hubris is the phenomenon of "glory by association." This form occurs when family members of the hubristic executive make appearances at the work site. At one time, this phenomenon was informally institutionalized in the social structure of many systems. Navy wives "wore the rank" of their husbands; spouses of individuals who were going through the selection process for being hired at the executive level were informally judged at social events put on for that purpose; and the boss's wife was accorded an appreciable amount of deference, rather than the respect genuinely deserved.

I, personally, remember one case where the teen-age son of a plant manager was allowed to speak down to company employees, and heaven help the employee who dared challenge this. Although there is little recent evidence of this dynamic still being an acceptable norm for a functioning organization, it still does exist in some organizations, for example, Dennis Kozlowski spending $2,000,000 of Tyco's profits on a company birthday bash for his wife on a Greek island.

7. Self-Image: The New Organizational Objective

Eventually, the hubristic leader's self-image becomes the organizational objective, plain, pure, and simple. If the leader is highly hubristic, then the purpose of all organizational effectiveness is to reinforce the leader's self-image. However, if hubris is just beginning to take hold for the first time, then the transition should be fairly obvious.

One of the attributes that separates the truly hubristic leader from the truly effective one is that the effective leader knows that a move up within the system means that his or her job is to transition from "sole contributor of good work" to "enabler of good work." The executive's prime function is to support and develop the essential skills in those below so that they can make the individual and/or team contributions necessary for the successful completion of the organization's objectives. It is safe to assume that most hubristic leaders today were, at one time, very effective leaders. That is, they were able to make the transition from "sole contributors" to "enablers of others" without much difficulty.

If hubris begins to take hold, the truly amazing phenomenon is that, once the leader has become an effective "enabler," the emphasis begins to shift back. With each passing day, the leader's self-perception increasingly becomes one of "sole contributor" once again. Eventually, when the leader is fully in the throes of hubris, the transition will have gone full circle—from being a "sole contributor" at the lower level; through becoming an effective "enabler of others" at the higher level; and ending with the self-perception of being *the* "sole contributor" at the highest level.

When this transition has been made, each accomplishment by an organizational individual or team is no longer measured against the template of, "How good is this result for the employee?" but rather, "How good is this outcome in terms of maintaining the importance of me?" Note that these two templates may not be mutually exclusive at all, particularly during the early onset of hubris. What is important, as with all things dealing with hubris, is being aware of which template is the dominant one.

Proven Coaching Interventions (Currently, There Aren't Any)

A client's or a boss's hubris is rarely, if ever, the direct subject of coaching. In most cases, the hubris is having a negative impact on the process, since it is a powerful factor in the working relationship between the client and the boss that is not being recognized.

In coaching managers or executives who seem to be suffering from hubris themselves, or who are inflicting its effects on others, the coach must be aware of the potential impact this has on the outcomes of the coaching endeavor. Coaching is truly an art form. Each practitioner does it his or her distinctive way, the situation in which the coaching occurs is always unique, and the client is always different, even when it's the same client in a new situation or at a different time. For this reason there can be no hard and fast "rules of engagement" or list of techniques that are bound to work.

The major skills that any coach brings to the work are awareness, good contact skills, and experience. If hubris is a suspected factor in the coaching process, then the coach would do well to consider the eight factors below and respond to any of those that might have relevance to the ongoing work. I believe these suggestions will assist any manager in working more effectively with his or her boss; however, these are critical concerns if the boss is in the throes of hubris. The eight factors are Hubris Doesn't Necessarily Mean Mean; Maintain a Moderate Profile; Be "Up-Front" Rather Than "Open" (Herman, 1974); If Appropriate, Accord Some Credit to the Boss; Err on the Side of Caution; No Surprises; Hubristic Doesn't Mean Mentally Ill; and Look for Other Opportunities.

While I am addressing all those who are engaged in coaching, I am going to address the client who may be working for a hubristic boss specifically, for the sake of simpler verbiage.

1. Hubris Doesn't Necessarily Mean Mean

It is reasonable to assume that, as hubris increases, mean-spiritedness will increase along with it. After all, as an executive becomes more and more convinced of his or her own state of perfection and/or moral superiority, the less tolerant that person becomes of those who do not agree with this conviction. Most cases of hubris that come to light are accompanied by myriad stories pertaining to the disrespect, harshness, threat, and humiliation heaped on those below the executive in the system.

There are some cases, on the other hand, where the hubristic manager simply condescends or sincerely supports those having less stature and understanding in the system. A strong tactical error can occur by not recognizing hubris simply for what it is and *then* noting what other attributes might be operative as well, for example, patronage, condescension, or harshness.

2. Maintain a Moderate Profile

One of the typical outcomes for a coach when working for a hubristic boss is playing down his or her own competence. *I am by no means suggesting that you should pander to a boss's ego needs;* however, there is something to be said for being somewhat circumspect. It is rare that a boss will recognize, much less "own," the condition of being hubristic. Given this, you will maintain a safer and more appreciated position by succeeding without being seen as threatening. The one time when it is relatively safe to come on strong is when your boss's objectives are being strengthened or image is being enhanced.

3. Be "Up-Front" Rather than "Open"

The old bromide, "Speak truth to power" is excellent advice. Get caught in a lie once by a boss and your credibility is gone forever and you become a liability rather than a resource. This is even more true if your boss is hubristic. I am going to suggest that being "open" with a hubristic boss can, at times, be just as disastrous for you as lying. Being open means that you disclose all of what you think or feel, and while this could situationally be a good thing from time to time, it could also lead to your downfall.

Rather than being open, I think it is far more realistic to be "up-front." Up-front means that you do not have to disclose things that you choose not to. However, anything that you do disclose can be fully counted on to be the case as you see it.

4. If at All Appropriate, Accord at Least Some of the Credit to the Boss

In many cases, giving your boss credit will be the appropriate thing to do, regardless of whether your boss is hubristic or not. If your boss is hubristic, it becomes an advantage to you to make sure that, if some credit is due, it is given. Not being accorded credit for providing support or resources can lead to the boss feeling threatened, unappreciated, or not recognized. Acknowledging the boss's contribution only takes a moment and can go a long way in keeping your working relationship safe and productive.

5. Err on the Side of Caution

Many bosses, and certainly most good ones, want to hear others' opinions because, after all, more information is better than less information. On the other hand, the more hubristic a boss becomes, the more he or she generally wants *confirmation, rather than information.* You owe it to your boss to provide data and opinions that may increase the chance of success or avoid a failure. The key is in how you present it. Rather than blurting out, "I think that if we proceed with this we're headed for the dumper," you might try something like, "I can see the possibility of at least one bad outcome if we proceed. Can I share this with you?" The rule of thumb is, "Avoid giving 'bad news' unless you have cleared the ground to do so."

6. No Surprises!

No boss likes surprises, and I'm talking about the "good" surprises as well as the bad. If your boss is hubristic, this factor becomes much more critical. Suppose, for example, after a meeting, one of your boss's peers comes up to him or her and says something like, "Congratulations on Jones closing the Digby account. That's quite a coup!" and this is the first time your boss has heard anything about it. The first thing this suggests is that other parts of the organization are better informed about what's happening in your department than your boss is. The second thing is that people inside the department are better informed than your boss is as well. I can't come up with a more paranoia-inducing scenario than this one, and, by the way, if you happen to be "Jones," you're probably in for a *very* rough time.

7. Hubristic Does Not Mean Mentally Ill

There seems to be a strong tendency in many people to try to explain away inappropriate behavior by attributing it to mental illness. Doing this is simple, it's easy, and you don't have to get worked up or go to the trouble of demanding accountability.

The capacity for hubris is a human tendency that is normally distributed in the population just like any other human capacity such as humor, anger, or nurturance. You are far better off recognizing it for what it is than you are trying to explain it away. By acknowledging it first, you are then in the position to determine the best way to deal with it.

8. Keep an Eye Out for Other Opportunities

Not every highly successful boss is a victim of hubris, and I would suggest that the great majority are not. Nevertheless, this still leaves a huge number who are. Being aware of the phenomenon is a necessary but not sufficient step for learning how to deal with it. In many cases, it is a relatively easy thing to do, being aware of the preceding seven factors.

On the other hand, hubris is a dynamic capacity. It doesn't stay where it is and it doesn't go away unless the boss experiences a solid observable failure. What this suggests is that hubris, in most cases, will get worse. Once you recognize that you are now working for a hubristic boss and are able to deal with it, it's still never a bad idea to keep your eyes open for other and better opportunities.

Summary and Conclusion

Historically, no other form of organizational dysfunction has had a longer or more devastating impact on leadership performance than has hubris. While occasionally mentioned in song and story, it has been almost totally ignored as an organizational dynamic. As long as its existence is ignored, it will, in the long run, continue to be *the* primary source of leadership and organizational failure.

Aside from OD, no other profession has the opportunity or the obligation to expose the dynamics and impact of hubris. As coaches, we have the competence, the insight, the ethical imperative, and the organizational access to at least begin to shed some light on this phenomenon. While dealing with the effects of hubris on those lower down in the system is a difficult task, the *real* challenge is to be able to confront the actual hubristic leader when we, as coaches, are aware of the condition in our client, and he or she is not.

References

Bateman, T., & Snell, S. (2002). *Management: Competing in the new era* (5th ed.). New York: McGraw-Hill.

Herman, S.M. (1974). The shadow of organization development. In J.W. Pfeiffer and J.E. Jones (Eds.), *The 1974 annual handbook for group facilitators.* San Francisco, CA: Pfeiffer.

Holy Bible. Proverbs (xvi: 18)

Karp, H.B. (1985). *Personal power: An unorthodox guide to success.* Lake Worth, FL: Gardner Press.

Karp, H.B., & Jackson, K.A. (2003). Hubris: A Gestalt alternative to groupthink. *Gestalt Review, 8*(1).

The Random House Dictionary. (1967). p. 690.

H.B. Karp, *Ph.D., LPC, is currently on the faculty of management at Hampton University, Hampton, Virginia, and is a licensed professional counselor in the state of Virginia. He consults in the areas of team building, conflict management, and executive coaching, specializing in Gestalt applications to individual growth and organizational effectiveness. Dr. Karp is a prolific writer, most notably being lead author of* Bridging the Boomer Xer Gap *(Davis-Black), which was the ForeWord Gold Winner for Best Book of 2002 in Business and Economics and received the Soundview Executive Summary Award for being one of the thirty best business books of 2002.*

Inside or Outside
The Partnerships of Internal and External Consultants
Beverly Scott and Jane Hascall

Summary

Although external and internal consultants have much in common, their different experiences and positioning in relation to the organization result in unique strengths and contrasting perceptions by their clients (Scott & Hascall, 2002). Their respective contributions and value vary according to the needs and viewpoints of clients, and their authority and credibility derive from different sources. In this article, the authors address the special challenges of working with large consulting firms, review the requirements for productive partnering between external and internal consultants, and offer advice to managers for maximizing the success of consulting projects.

External and internal consultants share the same role in helping their clients address problems and improve business and organization results; they both have a passion for the wisdom and expertise they bring to the organization, and they both have the ability to galvanize clients into action. Yet those of us who have spent years in both roles know there are significant differences in perspectives, challenges, and requirements. External consultants are often hired because they bring wisdom, objectivity, and expertise to the organization. They are seen as gurus or saviors bringing wise counsel. Internal consultants have expertise, but as organization insiders, their expertise is valued differently. In addition, as one former internal consultant suggested, "The difference is a matter of degree, but the biggest difference is in having a boss!"

"External practitioners need to provide a neutral perspective and to share their expertise. They need to know 'their stuff' and bring the wider worldview. Internals need to work with budget and political issues, anticipate potential obstacles and remove them, and know how and when to use an external, not just abdicate and turn the project over to the external. Sometimes internals are resentful because they don't get the opportunity to design and deliver. Where the internal adds value is in managing the process." (Susan Skjei, former internal OD manager and VP and chief learning officer at StorageTek; currently external)

The common skills and expertise of organizational consultants enable them to transition from one role to the other, but their differences can trip them up unexpectedly. This commonality may lead to competition between them when they work in the same organization; yet the differences can support a dynamic and successful partnership for the client. The challenges and requirements for each of these roles are different and often unclear from the other's vantage point. (See Table 1.) In this article, based on interviews of over seventy-five internal and external consultants, we will explore how organizations can utilize the value each brings and how internal and external consultants can maximize their partnership in working with joint clients.

"I was reminded during my time inside that when you are in the system you are part of the system—for better and for worse. Being inside inhibits your detachment. I think the main difference between internal and external consultants is

Table 1.   How to Decide Which to Use

When to Use External Consultants	When to Use Internal Consultants
To support development of strategy or facilitate corporate-wide initiatives or key priorities	To support implementation of strategic priority or intervention as an operational focus
Internal expertise does not reside within the organization	Organization possesses the needed internal expertise
Deep expertise is needed	Broad generalist knowledge is needed
An outside, neutral perspective is important	Knowledge of the organization and business is critical
New, risky alternatives require validation from an outside expert	Speaking the jargon or the language of the organization and the culture is important
Internal does not have status, power, or authority to influence senior management or the culture	A sensitive insider who knows the issues is needed
CEO, president, or senior leaders need coach, guide, or objective sounding board	Need to sustain a long-term initiative where internal ownership is important
Initiative justifies the expense	Cost is a factor
Project has defined boundaries or limits	Follow-up and quick access are needed

that the internal consultant is more focused on task and the external on process. Neither is 'better' than the other: In order to have strategic change you must have both." (Amanda Trosten-Bloom, Corporation for Positive Change, currently external, formerly internal)

"Executives are more likely to hear an idea from an external. They get more buy-in. Senior level executives prefer to hear from outsiders. Internals are employees and often executives don't want to hear from employees. An advantage of internals, however, is that she or he is familiar with the organization. Therefore, follow-up is easier and the internal can quickly give advice on a problem." (Keiko Kobayashi, currently external, formerly internal and manager for companies in Canada and the Middle East)

Contribution and Value

The external consultant is often viewed as having higher levels of expertise, experience, and credibility, especially if he or she is published, credentialed, and well-known. This gives the external more influence with and buy-in from senior level executives, who may prefer to hear from outsiders. Paying for services also implies the output is better or more valued. In addition to these perceived advantages, externals are frequently more up-to-date on the newest business thinking and new ways of working, and they bring the added value of a broader base of experience. With this broader experience, the external can provide benchmarking and best practices as well as insights into potential pitfalls learned from other clients. Externals are valued by clients for their outsider objectivity and ability to give tough feedback or to ask the difficult questions.

> "Externals are seen to have a value-add of higher levels of expertise than internals, though this is not often the case. When I was internal, the organization could not look past the title or my position in the company to hear my expertise. As an external, my recommendations are listened to." (Tricia Steege, Transformation Strategies, former internal)

Internal consultants, limited by perceptions and position in the organization, add a different value of in-depth knowledge of the business, the organization, and the management. This in-depth knowledge makes them particularly valuable on sensitive implementation of strategic change projects or culture transformation initiatives, managing processes or projects, and integrating or leveraging initiatives across the organization. Unfortunately, many organizations do not recognize the value of a strong and competent internal consulting function, so they hire less experienced or less competent junior consultants and place them in uninfluential lower positions in the hierarchy.

Use an Internal or External Consultant?

Because internal and external consultants add different value, clients can assess their needs and make the choice of which to use based on the contributions each makes. Table 1 suggests some criteria to use in making the best choice based on the recommendations from our interviews.

> "I worked with one organization that used its internal consultants at the corporate level as consultants to different business units while it saved the use of external consultants for high-level strategic consulting to the corporate leadership and/or for company-wide development of internal change agents. This model was very effective: It utilized the more cost-effective (yet still highly skilled and experienced) senior internal consultants as strategic partners to the leaders of business units and larger plants. The seniors developed the more junior internal consultants, who consulted to the plant and at team levels throughout the organization. These consultants were true consultants—they worked with the business units to help improve the effectiveness of those units. The external consultants, who were all highly respected in their fields, were used to stretch the thinking of the senior executives. Externals were not used as 'pairs of hands.'" (Marcelline Babicz, president of NewView International, former manager and internal)

Credibility and Authority

Although we have explored the differences in the value and contribution of internal and external consultants, much of the decision to utilize internals or bring in an outside firm seems to be based on the perceptions and opinions that senior management hold. When the internal consulting function is held in high esteem, and has respect and internal credibility, a decision to use external resources tends to be a more disciplined and rationale choice. Table 2 captures some of the similarities and differences between internal and external consultants.

In 1967, respected management thinker William Oncken proposed the notion that "Authority is whatever you possess at the moment that causes someone else to do what you want him to do at that moment" (1967, p. A4). Although Oncken's original context was management, we believe his four components of authority or credibility apply equally to consulting:

- The authority of *competence,* or expertise, prompts others to believe a consultant is knowledgeable and to follow his or her recommendations. Others will give only surface compliance and, "at worst, ignore or sabotage" a consultant who is not perceived to have competence. Although internal OD practitioners can possess very high levels of competence, externals seem to arrive

Table 2.   Comparison of External and Internal Consultants

Similarities	Differences	
	Internals	Externals
Knowledge of human systems, organization, and individual behavior	Accepted as a member of the "group," congruent with culture	Sees culture and organization with outsider perspective
Understanding the process of change	Has credibility as an insider	Has credibility as an outsider
Desire to be successful and recognized for the value they bring to the client	Knows organization and business intimately	Brings broader experience from other organizations
Commitment to learning	Can build long-term relationships; establish rapport more easily	Can confront, give feedback, take risks with senior management more easily
Passion about their work	Coordination and integration of project into ongoing activities	Focused involvement on a project that ends
Ability to influence and lead	Opportunities to influence, gain access, sit at the table as an insider	Once invited in as outsider, broader experience offers credibility, power, and influence
Skills to analyze needs and design interventions	Leverages and utilizes informal and formal organization structure	Can avoid or ignore the organization structure, move around organization to achieve results
Credibility or "authority"	Leads from position and character	Leads from competence (expertise) and (trust) personality
	Knows the cultural norms that should not be violated	Can acceptably challenge or violate the informal rules of the culture
	Knows the history, traditions, and where "bones are buried"	Seen as objective and not part of the problem
	Can take an advocacy role	Brings more objectivity, neutrality
	May be expected to be a broad generalist	Often seen a specialist with narrow expertise
	As a "one client" consultant, has a lot more "skin in the game"	If it doesn't work out here, can always move on to other clients

wearing the mantle of competence. This seems unfair and maddening to the internal and is not always reflective of reality for the external.

- The authority of *position* demands compliance and influences others to defer to those with greater power. Internals may and often do possess position power, depending on their organizational level. Externals rarely possess position power unless they arrive on the scene bearing a widely acclaimed reputation.

- The authority of *personality*, or behavior, makes it "easy to do business" with the consultant who establishes rapport with ease. Successful externals tend to be masters at this because they need to sell themselves to pay the bills; internals should be but are not always personable.

- The authority of *character*, or trust, is the consultant's "credit rating" with other people, based on integrity, reliability, honesty, loyalty, sincerity, personal morals, and ethics. It is the establishment of respect based on the trail of promises kept or broken, expectations fulfilled or forgotten, statements corroborated or disproved. The authority of character must be developed or "cultivated," based on one's track record. Internals tend to establish great authority of character; externals tend to have a tougher time establishing this component of authority. Marketing and selling services evokes suspicions of self-interest over the organization's interests. The authority of character, or trust, is the most difficult to establish, but once earned is the most powerful. But if trust is lost, it is very difficult to recover.

Applying Oncken's perspective reinforces the differences in perspective and context for internals and externals. Internals more often lead and exercise power through position and character, externals through competence and personality. When consultants work together on joint projects, clarity and understanding of these differences and the requisite skill sets required increases the prospects for success.

Partnerships

When the external is hired to work in an organization, misperceptions and confusion of roles can lead to breakdowns in collaboration, learning, and successful results for the organization. When the strengths of the internal consultant are recognized and valued by the external, and the internal is open to the learning and the leverage that can result from close collaboration with the external, a successful partnership can achieve significant results for the client. The experience of "being in it together" occurs when the internal's inside perspective and knowledge of the organization and the business are paired with the outside perspective and broader expertise of the external.

The advantage of this holistic view, as one consultant described it, "is that the internal knows the culture and where the dots need to be connected while the external brings the credibility of what has worked elsewhere and can be more daring." Partnership can be a real asset for the internal in the cross-fertilization of approaches and knowledge. Indeed, most internals expect to learn and be challenged by externals with specific expertise, fresh thinking, new ideas, and an impartial view. It is beneficial, too, to have someone with whom to bounce ideas around. From the organization's viewpoint, the internal-external partnership offers opportunity to leverage cost efficiencies, knowledge, and credibility.

Successful Partnerships

"What made the partnership a success . . . continuity was important to them. Telling the truth, being a woman of my word, honesty, establishing trust, having a realistic picture of the client system, knowing the client and knowing myself well enough to know when to bring in additional expertise. We had the intent of transferring ownership and facilitation of the work into the organization. I've never done exactly the same thing with them more than once; it has become theirs—the internals have taken over. We have not been afraid as a team to try things we haven't done before. Everybody's grown through our work together." (Amanda Trosten-Bloom, Corporation for Positive Change, former internal)

"We worked hard to ensure a holistic program rather than a parade of external experts with internal people thrown in." (Marguerite Foxon, principal performance technologist, Motorola)

"Flexibility and honesty between internal and external consultants were critical; the relationship developed during the year of working together as our business priorities changed, needs changed around pace, content, etc. Trust strengthened the relationship during the time we worked together. We talked a lot both formally with others and informally one on one; this was very important. The consultant was skilled at listening and taking what I was trying to communicate and turning it into a workable solution that kept everything aligned. I really valued their impartiality and ability to challenge our thinking and guide us to a successful completion." (Jo-Anne Miller, learning and development manager, StorageTek, London)

Partnership can be even more important when the initiative involves the complexity of other national or ethnic cultures. Drawing on as wide and deep a pool of resources as possible is critical. For change issues and initiatives implemented globally, it is imperative to have a consultant with experience in the culture facilitate buy-in by the local region. Either the internal or the external may bring the sensitivity and awareness required to tailor and manage the cultural differences. Other benefits of utilizing a cross-cultural partnership include greater appreciation and understanding of differences in work ethics, cultural norms, and language, especially jargon and slang.

Poor Partnerships

However, several conditions may undermine the opportunity for partnership:

- Internal consultants, as external Allon Shevat suggests, must recognize that they may not be in a position or have enough organizational influence to lead a major change initiative. It's their internal political position that is limiting, and not necessarily their capabilities.

- Senior management may not understand the value of the ties internals have within the organization to support a change effort, and thus they fail to support a partnership with the external firm they bring in.

- Internals left out of the contracting process may feel resentful, threatened, and marginalized, resulting in a lack of commitment. This may lead to alignment with the old way and with clients threatened by the impending change and result in potential for undermining and sabotage.

- Externals are often seen as arrogant, exclusive, judgmental; in turn, internals may be perceived as ineffective, incompetent, and "poor losers."

- Externals ignore or go around the internal function, promoting themselves solely to senior management.

- Weak internal functions may not have the capacity to successfully lead change projects.

    "The primary internal was a very scattered, immature person who was dealing with significant challenges in terms of his capacity to deal with the world. The result was an inability to focus, take in, or act on the advice of the consultant. The project was held hostage to the client's idiosyncrasies." (Amanda Trosten-Bloom, Corporation for Positive Change, former internal)

    "Five years later it (the change) still doesn't work, despite a lot of tweaking and whacking and much internal communication, none of which works. There was a lot of work for independent externals afterwards, 'the [Large Firm] aftermarket,' and it is hard to find anyone who will admit to having been part of the exercise." (Line manager at an international financial institution)

Working with Large Consulting Firms

Most internal consultants report that partnering and working with large consulting firms is difficult. Large firms have their own way of doing things and tend not to be flexible enough to incorporate other approaches and ideas. Some internals complain that the large firms use academic models that are not based in real-world business applications and that they apply these models without doing up-front diagnosis. (This is the "if the only tool you have is a hammer, every problem is a nail" syndrome.) Most firms approach projects from an American or Anglo model and, despite their claims of a global presence, the models are seldom adapted to fit local or regional culture. Many internal consultants have experience with large firms in which the end objectives were not met, the budget was substantially exceeded, and the credibility of the internal consultant was undermined or ruined. The arrogance, incompetence, and high fees lead many to conclude that working with large consulting firms is hardly worth it, despite a few pockets of excellence based more on individual talents than consulting firm excellence.

> "The most challenging and painful experiences I have had were when we were working in partnership with large external consulting groups. I have been through them all. In every case, I have had a negative experience. There never truly is a partnership, even though we contracted up-front. We did role clarification: 'What we need from you is. . .' and 'What do you need from us?' Some were not even willing to do that. They did not have the same accountability as we had. And we even charged internally for our services. They practically had a blank check, but the same standards were not being applied to the large external groups.
>
> "We were resource-deficient, and I often encouraged management to hire them because it was too big for us to handle ourselves. They would be given lots of attention by higher management, who would just lie down and let them roll over them. In almost every case, we were disappointed. Upper management would get disenthralled, and the internal group would have to come in and clean up the mess. I went through four or five of these, always with the same outcome." (Eddie Reynolds, consultant, executive and organization development, former internal consultant with high-technology industry [Scott, 2000])

> "I walked into a new division as one of three internals to find that a large external firm had already been involved for over six months. The external firm had convinced the organization to pay for two full-time consultants, five days per week for the previous six months. The internals in the division were very weak and had gone along with this because the division leadership wanted it. The external firm was supposed to be leading the organization through a process of re-engineering, improving cost effectiveness, and overall organization improvement. Turns out they just steered a bunch of teams to the conclusion that 'asset teams' were the way to run the business. This consulting firm was the only one that had experience in converting traditional organizations to asset teams in this industry,

so they led the conversion. The lead consultant was a marketing guy who had no knowledge of organizational theory or organization behavior. All he knew was his company's standard methodology for converting to asset teams.

"The disaster was that the organization structure was changed, but not much else. After the externals left, we—the internals—had to try to make it work. The savings touted by the consultants were temporary. The organization learned nothing from this fiasco, because the upper management moved on to other things before the lack of improvement really showed itself. This, in my experience, is one of the biggest reasons disastrous interventions don't create learning: The negative effects may take a while to show, and by then the perpetrators have left or been promoted. By then, it's almost impossible to trace the negatives back to the specific intervention." (Marcelline Babicz, president of New View International, LLC, former manager and internal consultant)

Requirements for Productive Partnerships

Partnership is the key to success when externals and internals work on joint projects. Internal Susan Curtis, director, Work Force Development at StorageTek, states, "I believe it is the attitude of the consultant and the internal staff that make the difference. If both approach the work from a limited pie perspective, there is a tendency to grab what I can for me. However, if the perspective is 'there's plenty for everyone,' the relationship has an opportunity to flourish and grow."

> "I've worked closely with the VP of HR at the oldest and largest retail products company in Canada. We have an amazingly open, honest partnership. She understands the internal politics and I provide the credibility and processes to work with the CEO to build the leadership team. We have collaborated many times to create customized programs . . . our relationship is beautiful. We have total trust and respect for one another. We literally didn't have any conflicts. I supported her, both professionally and as a personal coach; and she would guide me regarding how to best engage with the senior team. I had a ten-year relationship with the CEO, but I still really needed her guidance and support to deal with some of the other members of the leadership team." (Mac Carter, Turning Points Inc. external consultant)

Based on our own experience and the advice of many consultants, we offer the following advice.

For Externals

- Remember who your client is.

- Recognize the enormous value of the internal as ally rather than neutral observer or, worse, enemy.

- Respect the internal consultant's authority, expertise, and role in the organization.

- Communicate honestly and frequently.

- Be clear about and deliver on your promises.

- Value the internal's deep knowledge of the organization.

- Become clear about and respect personal boundaries.

- Stay apolitical and maintain objectivity.

- Maintain the highest of ethical standards.

- Leave the organization better off when you depart than when you entered.

- Transfer skills/knowledge to internals and the client system.

- Bring the organization the benefits of your knowledge of the wider world.

For Internals

- Go after partnership with externals.

- Ensure that management understands the value and expertise of internal consulting.

- Be politically neutral or politically savvy.

- Don't be offended, don't whine about not being included, and don't act out resentment in petty ways.

- Recognize that the external consultants become stakeholders in the organization and that they are under the gun to perform also.

- Learn everything you can from externals.

- Help clients understand that they need to play ball and join in the change process.

- Be clear about your role and competencies before confronting the challenges of large-scale change that is planned and managed by an external firm.

- Consider using small firms that specialize in partnership with internal consultants.

- When managing an external firm, some suggestions are

    ○ Define expectations for the external and internal partners in the project.

    ○ Discuss and determine how conflicts and differences will be resolved.

    ○ Manage the scope of the project very carefully.

    ○ Plan frequent communication; build in scheduled checkpoints.

"Establishing the contract took up most of the time. The conditions were trust, open and honest communication (no matter how harmful that communication is—giving the organization the shock it needs), buy-in from executive membership and key people around the business who can influence, a clear understanding of expectations both ways (often things go wrong when you only get expectations from the client and not the consultant), limitations of budget, resources, and knowledge (I expect external experts to challenge me), and respect for each other's roles. By far the most productive behaviors in this relationship were challenging the status quo, listening, and using real-time feedback and questioning." (Faran Johnson, VP of OD, First Data Corporation, based in London and York, UK)

When internal/external partnerships fail, there are missed opportunities for the transfer of skills and knowledge, and a failed implementation can mean disastrous results for the organization and its employees. When externals rather than internals are managing the process, the final insult is a departing consulting firm that leaves the internal function to "clean up the mess." On the other hand, a successful partnership draws on the strengths of both the internal and the external. The organization benefits and the consultants all learn from the partnership.

Advice for Managers

A successful outcome is based in support from senior management and key clients in the organization. Internal and external consultants offer the following advice for managers to contribute to successful initiatives involving internal-external partnerships:

- Ensure and accept the time that is required for the organization and employees to buy in and accept radical change.

- Stay open to the expertise and knowledge of internal consultants, regardless of title and position in the hierarchy.

- Recognize that just because consultants come from a large well-known firm doesn't ensure their competence in leading the human side of the change process.

- Keep your agreements with both the internal and external consultants. When you do not, it not only undermines the credibility of the consultants, but also, more importantly, may result in a failed project and wasted resources and a damaged reputation for the manager who sponsored the project.

- Get input from internal consultants before hiring externals. There are too many examples of externals not delivering what the company needs.

- Communicate expectations and hold consulting firms accountable to partner with the internal function.

- Ensure that the external firm is accountable to and managed by an internal person with authority and knowledge of organizational change and the management of consulting contracts.

- Always debrief with "lessons learned" at the close of a major project. Involve all the key players, external and internal. Be sure key learnings are recorded and shared for future use.

> "I had one partnership experience with the best will in the world. We worked together well, did all the right things, but we were sabotaged by the senior executives. They did not follow through on their promises and did not do what they said they would do. The result for the external was not being asked back again; it was much more dire for the internal, whose credibility was damaged and who eventually had to leave the company." (External consultant on global business issues; worked internally at six multinational organizations)

Summary

Successful involvement of consultants in organizational change projects is increased by appropriately choosing whether internal or external consulting resources will contribute the most value. Indeed, in many cases, a partnership that leverages the advantages of both internal and external often provides the best value to the organization, provided that senior management supports and endorses it.

References

Oncken, W. (1967, July 10). The authority to manage. *Training Bulletin, 1*, A4. For a complete, updated copy of the article, please contact The William Oncken Corporation, 18601 LBJ Freeway, Suite 520, Mesquite, TX 75150, 972–613–2084, Onckencorp@aol.com.

Scott, B. (2000). *Consulting on the inside: An internal consultant's guide to living and working inside organizations.* Alexandra, VA: American Society for Training and Development, p. 54.

Scott, B., & Hascall, J. (2002). *Inside or outside: The partnerships of internal and external consultants.* Global Business and Technology Association (www.gbata.com).

Beverly Scott, *an organization consultant and executive coach, brings clarity, focus, integrity, and a sense of purpose to her work. She has worked as both an internal and an external consultant. She has written many articles and two books. Her latest book,* Consulting on the Inside: An Internal Consultant's Guide to Living and Working Inside Organizations, *published in 2000 by the American Society for Training and Development, is a best-seller.*

Jane Hascall, *a group facilitator, trainer, and speaker since 1974, is an expert in group process, personal and organizational planning, team building, conflict resolution, and merger integration. In recent years she has presented at ten professional conferences in Europe and North America and co-authored three articles on internal and external consulting. She is listed in the 2003 edition of* Who's Who in America.

Making a Difference
The Client–Consultant Relationship
Mohandas K. Nair

Summary

Clients approach consultants to service needs that they are unable to take care of themselves. They expect the consultant to walk that extra mile to satisfy their requirements and to make a difference to the organizational bottom line. For the consultant, the task is daunting. He or she may have to overcome several technical and non-technical hurdles, including non-availability of data, mis-information, prejudices, indifferences, and possible animosity, before the client accepts the consultant and the consultant's credentials. The consultant therefore must do ample groundwork before tackling an assignment. It is not just about technical know-how, but also about human skills.

This article provides some guidelines to the consultant on how to really make a difference for the client.

A client has very specific needs when he or she approaches a consultant for help. While contracting with an organization, the consultant deals with a particular individual or a group of people who may not adequately convey the organization's needs, so the consultant must collect the necessary data to see the complete picture.

Understanding the real needs of the client is very important. It is equally important to understand how the members of the organization relate to one another. Socratic questioning can be a powerful technique for use here. The consultant should ask questions and continue to follow up on the responses until he or she is satisfied that the root problem has been determined. The consultant may feel tempted to short-circuit this needs assessment process and begin work. That would, however, be a mistake.

During the process, the client's needs may change, and the consultant has to be attuned to this possibility. The client may have an unclear picture of what he or she wants to happen, so the consultant must probe for details.

All consultants know the drill. Whatever structure or method they adopt should be tailored to the unique needs of the client.

The consultant may not possess the complete set of skills and the necessary knowledge base to tackle every assignment. He or she may want to network with specialists to ask for advice on solving some types of problems. The consultant should be able to generate synergy among members of the client group and motivate them to contribute positively to the organization's growth.

The key elements of a successful consultant-client relationship are addressed below.

Winning Over the Client

The client has the best understanding of the organization's system, processes, and operations. He or she may be possessive about this knowledge and may not want to divulge information. It is in the consultant's interest to learn everything possible from the client and to use whatever skills and knowledge are available. You will need to make careful preparations to win over the client and elicit useful information. For this, you will need to educate the client about the assignment and train him or her to look at issues from a different perspective. The client needs to understand his or her role in the transformation and know the benefits that can accrue in the process.

Creating Synergy

A consultant must treat the client as a member of the team. For all practical purposes, the consultant is working in his or her own organization with his or her own team members—sharing experiences, ideas, fears, happiness, etc. This creates a bond that brings out the best in both the consultant and his or her teammates in the client organization. The process builds synergy and enables excellence in the output.

This is the reason for bringing you, the consultant, into the team—as a catalyst for change and building excellence.

Enabling Transition

As a consultant, you must understand the client's urgency and desire to achieve quick solutions to his or her problems. Remember that the client will have to work with the solution you create after you have completed the assignment. One of your goals should be to ready the client to continue to implement the work you've begun together, not to become a permanent fixture in the client organization yourself.

You are only a facilitator and have but a brief sojourn with the client. Build confidence in your clients that they can manage their processes by themselves. Make yourself redundant as soon as possible. Think of yourself as a lamppost—the client should use you as the light you shed, not lean on you.

Stirring Up Passion

Passion drives; passion excites. Without passionate involvement of both the consultant and the client, no assignment can be successful. Stir the client's passion by painting a bright and colorful picture of the future, but don't go overboard with your promises. Get management enthused about the prospective changes and help them to percolate the vision to every level. Make your passion for your work evident through regular client interactions, genuine concern for the client's well-being, and enthusiastic encouragement of the client's initiatives. The client will be buoyed by your passion and enthusiasm and will happily assist you in the assignment.

Being Empathic

A consultant can be a better facilitator if he or she can "get into the client's shoes." However, this is easier said than done. The "shoes" include the experiences of all members of the client organization, too numerous to understand, correlate, and define. Have an open mind, ask questions, and try to understand the client's feelings; listen actively, and be a keen observer of whatever is happening around you. Along the way, provide feedback about your perceptions of what is happening and dig for genuine answers to your queries. Being seen as trustworthy helps in this process.

It is very rare when the client provides the consultant with all the requisite information at the beginning of the assignment. Often what information there is is not in the desired format. The client's written information may also be different from what you expect and may be at variance with other practices within the organization.

It requires a lot of skill and patience on the consultant's part to sort the information. You have to empathize with the client and be patient when attempting to collect information you want.

Facilitating the Change Process

Train the client to solve his or her problems. If the client is confident in his or her ability to solve problems, the change will be greatly enhanced. "Teach them to fish" and enable them to blend what they already know with your new ideas. Help clients to learn and to develop themselves. Only then can they grow and, in turn, provide excellent services to their customers.

Overcoming Prejudices

One of your most daunting tasks is to stay free of internal politics and prejudices. Individuals in power are bound to try and exert their influence over you and may openly voice their displeasure at some of the changes you suggest. It's a tough task to be objective and remain focused on the project without upsetting the client. Remind yourself that your task is not to please a section of the clientele but to help the organization realize its goals, and that this may require you to make some unpopular changes.

Being Professional

One also has to be very discreet while discussing confidential matters with the client. Do not betray the client's trust by using information you have learned to win somebody else's favor. Obtain permission from the client before using anything he or she has told you.

Conclusion

A consultant's association with a client need not be a one-time affair or end in acrimony if the consultant exercises sufficient discretion during the course of the assignment. The entire process of change can be a pleasant transition rather than a painful experience for the client. The guidelines discussed above will help the consultant to maintain a healthy relationship with the client and help him or her realize his or her goals.

Mohandas K. Nair *freelances as an HRD consultant and trainer. He has an engineering background; his early experiences were in industrial engineering, both in industry and in consultancy. He has published various articles in newspapers, journals, and campus magazines and has also published two books:* Thoughts to Live By *and* Management: From the Experts. *His vision is "To make a positive impact on every person I meet and 'touch' and in the process make them aware of their potential."*

Accelerating the Project Lifecycle
The Partnership of Facilitation and Project Management
Tammy Adams and Jan Means

Summary

When faced with the need for change, businesses struggle with issues such as project speed, complexity, deliverable quality, and ownership of results within the organization. Incorporating facilitated work sessions into the project lifecycle to produce specific deliverables accelerates creation of the deliverable, contributes to process and deliverable quality, and ensures early ownership of results.

The following paper describes the context for facilitated working sessions and how they relate to complex business projects. It lists the benefits of using facilitated work sessions, provides a checklist to recognize when facilitated work sessions are most beneficial, and introduces five common types of facilitated work sessions, showing where they are typically applied within a project to affect speed and quality.

The Way Things Are

In a recent book on the subject of productivity, George Eckes comments on a study that finds that "the majority of time project teams fail; the primary root cause is poor team dynamics. . . . A more common stumbling block is how a team conducts its work, and the dynamics of the team. Thus, it is our hope that we can review the keys to improving what, for many, is an elusive target—having groups of individuals work together to achieve what they could not achieve alone" (2003, p. 2).

Yet this awareness regarding the effects of team dynamics and people challenges on projects is far from new. In 1987 Tom DeMarco and Timothy Lister published a work that pointed out that the major problems in accomplishing project work are not technology-based or task-based, but rather people-based. Our ability to effectively manage projects to successful completion is much more about tapping into the collective knowledge of *people* than about managing to a predefined project methodology and set of tasks.

Recently, Best Practices, LLC (2000) conducted a benchmarking survey to be a directional indicator of project management trends. The study was designed to check out the project performance of companies that are renowned for their project management operations. Most of the companies surveyed tend to conduct more than one hundred IT-related projects a year, with 21 percent conducting more that 150 business projects per year requiring IT components. Findings regarding the most significant causes of project delays included the following:

- Communication and planning factors, including lack of proper communication and cross-organization input;

- Scope creep;

- Incomplete business requirements; and

- Inadequate input from technology resources during early phases was noted 26 percent of the time.

All of these have their basis in people and their ability to communicate, make decisions, and share information throughout the project cycle. Choice of project methodology, or use of a non-standard project methodology, was rarely cited as the cause for project delays (5 percent).

The Context for Change

Any company that intends to remain healthy and competitive in an increasingly global and electronic marketplace must be willing to change, and it must do so in a timely and resource-effective manner. Too much change or change poorly conceived and administered is just as damaging as clinging to the status quo. But you already know that because, in one way or another, you're involved with projects, and projects are *all* about change.

So let's focus on *how change is accomplished* within organizations. For all but the smallest alterations in direction, change requires resources—time, people, funding, and supporting methods and tools. Substantive improvements and changes within a business are implemented via project initiatives. And that's where we begin.

Consider an ideal business world, one in which a business has a vision and mission that fit squarely into the marketplace it intends to serve. Business strategies are developed, tested, and adopted. Operational plans are developed to support these strategic objectives (and regulatory requirements) and create program initiatives, which carry out these plans. Program initiatives have specific goals and measurable targets. Within programs, projects are established to achieve selected goals and targets. Implemented results provide benefits that link back to programs, operational plans, and business strategies. We measure our effectiveness, identify what we've learned from the experience, and begin the cycle again.

Let's look at a single project within this change cycle. Don't be fooled into thinking that the project lives as an island unto itself. It was spawned by a business case and will ultimately implement a solution that will be held accountable to achieve the objectives of that business case.

As shown in Steps 1 through 6 of Figure 1, the project lifecycle starts with an idea, an opportunity for business change, and continues through subsequent phases to validate the opportunity, perform business analysis, define and build the solution, and, finally, implement the solution, at which point the project ends. Transition is complete. Ultimately, the business owns the solution and continues to monitor performance, assess learnings, and recognize when the next change is needed.

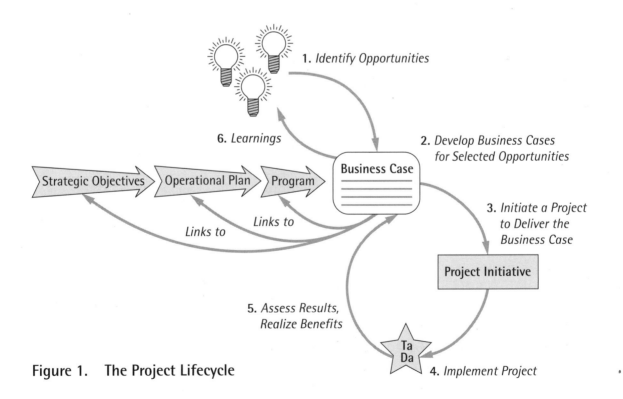

Figure 1.   The Project Lifecycle

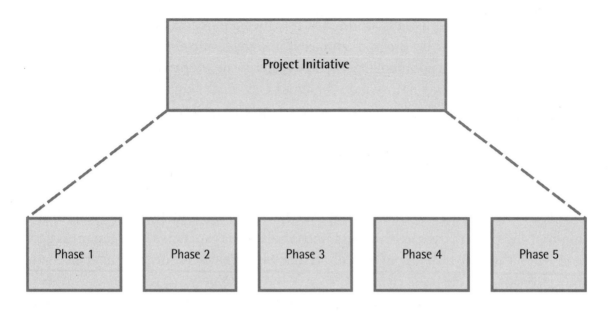

Figure 2.   Project Lifecycle Phases

To achieve this, project management methodologies organize project work into distinct phases of activity that accomplish a specific set of outputs. These chunks of activity, typically referred to as phases (see Figure 2), have meaning within the project methodology—accomplishing cohesive sets of work or providing convenient endpoints for business approval and funding decisions.

Whether your project lifecycle has four phases of work or nine phases of work is of less significance than *what you are required to produce* along the way. Every project must have certain fundamental deliverables, such as:

- A clearly defined scope;

- A clearly defined set of solution requirements;

- A clearly defined plan for implementation; and

- A clearly defined set of measurable objectives with which the business will track success.

These outputs transcend the somewhat artificial partitioning of project work into phases.

The project world, even in the most ideal setting, is complex. Multiple projects are active at any given point in time and vie for limited resources. Projects can be interdependent or multi-phased, adding difficulty to execution. Timelines are critical. Getting anything done can be as difficult as changing tires on a moving car.

And since none of us work in an ideal setting, our project experiences are filled with challenges beyond what we can list here. In the real world, projects don't always fit neatly into this model. Some projects should never have been started at all, while others should have been started much sooner. Some project sponsors are engaged and prepare the path for success, while others detach—to the detriment of the project team. Direction can be fuzzy, targets less than well-defined, resources unavailable or inadequate. But there's always a deadline. These are the cards that the project manager is dealt. And we do our best to work with them.

Facilitation in Support of Projects

It is into this setting that we introduce facilitation in support of projects. Facilitation is a discipline that enables the bringing together of people to accomplish a specific outcome in a determined period of time. And its application to projects, especially information technology projects, is not new.

In the mid-1970s, Chuck Morris of IBM embraced an innovative way to get groups of people together to design and implement distributed systems. This application of facilitation techniques birthed Joint Application Design (JAD) work sessions, during which business and technology professionals came together to jointly define requirements for design of computer systems. Use of facilitated group techniques (JADs) reduced time by 40 percent while improving the quality of design results. Fewer coding errors were made, and testing cycles improved accordingly.

However, the creative application of facilitated group work sessions in support of project initiatives has not been widely practiced within traditional project approaches. Facilitation within the project lifecycle is a new application of a proven concept, which supports project delivery by providing specialized skills and techniques that focus on people and access their collective knowledge. Facilitation enables us to engage the right people throughout the project effort to obtain the joint input of business and technology experts at the right time to build the right work products.

Several of our clients found that introducing facilitated work sessions into the project has a two-stage effect on acceleration. The first point of acceleration is realized when building the targeted deliverable, which is the focus of the work session. A second point of acceleration is noted downstream, where this deliverable is used in later project phases. The quality of this deliverable can eliminate rework in later phases, thus accelerating the project further.

Is this the only way of accelerating projects and introducing quality and ownership? Absolutely not. But does it work? Absolutely. Capers Jones, in his 2000 study of "Software Assessments, Benchmarks, and Best Practices," found that facilitated working sessions provide the following project benefits.

Tangible benefits include:

- Reduction of the risk of scope creep from 80 percent down to 10 percent;

- Acceleration in the early project lifecycle phases (including Scope Initiation, Planning, and Definition) by 30 to 40 percent; and

- Reduction of the overall project elapsed time and workforce effort by 5 to 15 percent.

Intangible benefits are similarly impressive and include:

- Ownership of results;

- Improved quality;

- Improved working relationships; and

- Shared decision making, which yields informed decisions and support of these decisions.

What Is a Facilitated Work Session?

So what is a facilitated work session? It's an event (usually ranging from one to three days) that brings a cross-functional project team together to build a specific project deliverable or achieve specific project goals. These work sessions have the following core characteristics:

- *They have a purpose that is aligned to project objectives.* The facilitated work session must have a set of clear objectives that fit within the work and outputs required by the project.

- *They are systematic.* The work session has a well-defined approach and structure. Preparation, work session delivery, and follow-up activities are all part of the work session process, with clear roles and responsibilities.

- *They are collaborative.* This is not a visit to a doctor's office or a trip to see an attorney. The participants do not show up so that an expert can tell them what to do. The participants *are* the experts and are led by a *neutral* facilitator who seeks the input and full involvement of all participants to achieve the objectives of the work session.

- *They encourage discovery.* The work session does not introduce "the answer" and then drive for acceptance. It is a place of discovery where the ideas and opinions of the participants contribute to exploring and embracing the best outcome for the business situation.

- *They create substantive outputs.* Work sessions must create high-quality outputs that are specific to the needs of the project. This is not an encounter group. This is not a discussion group. This is a work group. Group dialogue and interaction lead to creative decision making, which in turn is captured in appropriate deliverables as required by the project.

- *They promote accountability.* Decisions within project work sessions are made by consensus. This does not mean unanimity; rather it means that all participants are willing to support the decision 100 percent within and outside of the work session setting. They are accountable for the decisions they make and their resulting impacts on the business.

Recognizing the Need

Are we proposing that every project, no matter its complexity or purpose, should utilize facilitated work sessions? No. Then how do you know when a facilitated work session would be beneficial?

We've analyzed the projects we have worked on with our clients to determine which ones gained the most value from facilitated work sessions and found some common characteristics. If you can answer yes to any of the following questions, a facilitated work session will be a valuable contributor to the success of your project.

- Does your project effort *cross multiple lines of business* or multiple departments within the business?

- Is your project tied to a *critical timeline* that allows little or no slippage?

- Is your project one of the top ten *strategic initiatives* of the company or division?

- Is your project attempting to accomplish something that is *new* to your company?

- Is your project resurrecting something that was *tried before and was unsuccessful?*

- Does your project require *input of experts* who are unavailable to participate full-time (or on a regular basis) with your project team?

- Will your project result in changes that require broad *socialization* or group *consensus*?

- Are you experiencing *scope creep or* having difficulty defining *clear requirements* from the team?

- Are you operating in a *geographically dispersed project environment?*

Conversely, if your project scope is small and requirements are relatively uncomplicated in nature, or the project is not following a critical timeline, is less visible from a strategic viewpoint, or is something you've done over and over again, and you have a relatively small team who are co-located, then facilitated work sessions may not be of great benefit to your project. But even for these types of projects, we encourage you to find a way to incorporate expert knowledge into your project and to communicate information and decisions throughout the project team.

Types of Work Sessions

Although facilitated work sessions can be used for many purposes, we will focus on five core work session types that support the following:

- The building of several key deliverables that you would find in any project methodology;

- The ability to assess risks, and

- The ability to meet critical progress checkpoints along the way.

The five core work session types follow:

1. *Project Charter Work Session.* This work session starts you off on the right foot. It develops a shared understanding of the need or problem being addressed by the project effort and how it's being handled in the current environment. It level-sets the team on the work performed to date. And it defines the scope of the project, establishes the purpose and objectives, and uncovers impacts and dependencies so that informed decisions can be made about potential benefits, costs, and resourcing.

2. *Process Analysis and Design Work Session.* Business processes depict how work is done. Once scope has been established, the process analysis and design work session enables an understanding of how work is currently accomplished, compares this to customer expectations and business targets, explores points of breakdown, identifies opportunities for change, and redefines how work should be accomplished in the future. The roles and responsibilities involved in the process are defined, and initial expectations regarding supporting technology are captured. Process design also ensures that critical measurement points are factored in so that performance can be monitored and maintained.

3. *Business Requirements Work Session.* This work session gives substance to the solution. Thus far in the project, we have a clearly defined scope and redesigned work processes—the basic skeleton of the solution. The business requirements work session puts meat on the bones by defining *what* the business needs, not yet *how* the solution will be accomplished. The result is a clear, unambiguous definition of requirements for the project scope. All types of requirements needed to support the business solution are defined here. This includes requirements for supporting technology, as well as requirements pertaining to security needs, performance, people (training), and process (policy decisions).

4. *Risk Assessment Work Session.* The risk assessment work session promotes the careful analysis of project, business, process, and customer risks. Potential risks are rated with respect to severity, probability of occurrence, and ability to detect the effects of the risk. Causes are explored, and mitigating actions are identified. For the highest risks, contingency plans may also be created.

5. *Work-in-Progress Review Session.* Work-in-progress reviews provide key checkpoints on project progress. They can be inserted into the project prior to specific project milestones or phase completion to ensure that the project is on track, that deliverables are synchronized, that project dependencies and risks are being monitored, and that all team members and pertinent stakeholders understand what is being delivered.

Where Do Facilitated Work Sessions Fit Within the Project Lifecycle?

Facilitated work sessions can be applied at many points within the project lifecycle. The key is to recognize *what* needs to be delivered. Let's look at where these five work session types typically fit into the project. For illustration purposes, we'll show two project lifecycle examples. The first depicts a project lifecycle with four generically named phases (see Figure 3).

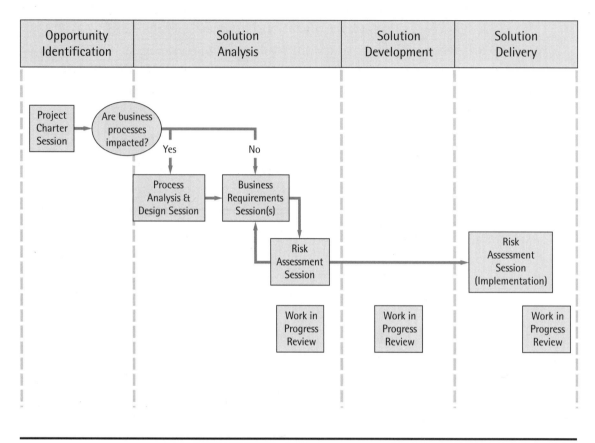

Project Phase	Purpose of Phase
Opportunity Identification	Define the opportunity, objectives, and targets, explore feasibility, establish the initial business case, set the scope of the project effort, and establish the project team and stakeholders.
Solution Analysis	Define the change. Design business processes and supporting roles. Establish requirements for people, process, and technology. Determine what will be measured.
Solution Development	Finalize solution design, prototype if appropriate, build out the solution, test, validate, and prepare for implementation.
Solution Delivery	Ready the organization, roll out the solution, internalize the change, and monitor performance.

Figure 3. Sample Project Lifecycle

The second example (see Figure 4) is specific to the Six Sigma methodology for business improvement and breaks the project into phases that parallel the Six Sigma DMAIC Lifecycle.

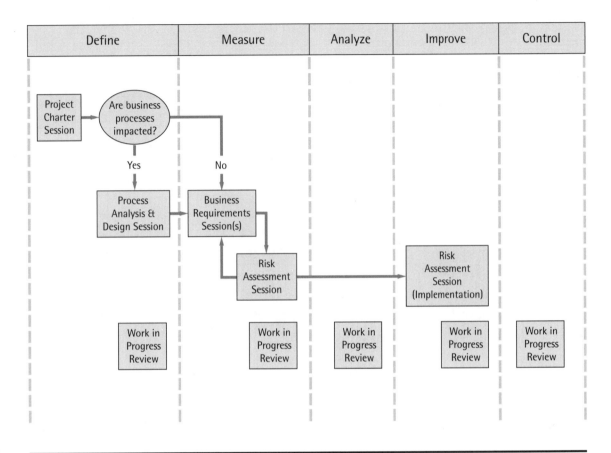

Project Phase	Purpose of Phase
Define	Establish the project goals and targets based on internal and external customer needs and expectations.
Measure	Understand current business ability to meet objectives and targets, and establish relevant, reliable measures. Define the requirements for the desired state.
Analyze	Determine the gaps that exist between current performance and desired state, and formulate the solution(s).
Improve	Build, validate, and implement the solution.
Control	Internalize the change. Monitor and manage performance to achieve objectives and meet targets.

Figure 4.   Six Sigma Example

In both of these examples, work sessions are inserted into the project phases *at the point where the corresponding deliverable makes sense.*

- The Project Charter work session yields a clear definition of project scope and so should be performed early in the project lifecycle.

- A Process Analysis and Design work session is used when business processes will be changing as a result of the project effort. Hold these work sessions first, since they lay the necessary foundation for successful definition of business requirements.

- Conduct a Business Requirements work session after the Project Charter has been finalized if no Process Assessment is being performed. Otherwise, wait until analysis of the process has been completed.

- Discover risks while analysis is still in progress by convening a Risk Assessment work session. As risks are explored, it is quite common to identify risks and corresponding mitigating factors that lead to additional requirements. As you approach implementation, again convene a Risk Assessment work session to identify new risks that may have emerged that are specifically related to testing and implementation.

- Throughout the project, convene Work-in-Progress review sessions prior to phase checkpoints to socialize and validate key deliverables, confirm integration of outputs, communicate resolution of issues, and verify project progress.

Conclusion

Realize that your project is likely one of many within the organization and will be competing for limited resources. Facilitated work sessions can enable the effective use of resources by pulling together the right people at the right time to create the right output. Joint development and joint ownership of the results paves the way for successful implementation and internalization of the change. Recognize when facilitated work sessions add the greatest value to a project and use them.

Insert facilitated work sessions into your project lifecycle intelligently. Use them when collaboration adds value and the resulting deliverable is needed. As a guide, use Table 1 for an "at-a-glance" look at where work sessions might be best placed within the project lifecycle.

Table 1.   At-a-Glance: Where Work Sessions Work

Deliverable Generated or Activity Supported	Work Session Type	Typical Phase Within Generic Project Lifecycle	Typical Phase Within Six Sigma Project Lifecycle
Project Scope	*Project Charter*	Opportunity Identification	Define
Business Process Design or Redesign	*Process Analysis and Design*	Solution Analysis	Define
Business Requirements for People, Business Processes, and Technology Support	*Business Requirements*	Solution Analysis	Measure
Project, Business, or Customer Risks Identified and Mitigating Actions Defined	*Risk Assessment*	Solution Analysis	Measure or Analyze
Potential Process Failure Points Identified and Mitigating Actions Defined	*Risk Assessment*	Solution Analysis	Measure or Analyze
Risk Checkpoint Prior to Implementation	*Risk Assessment*	Solution Development or Solution Delivery	Improve
Check on Project Progress	*Work-in-Progress Review*	All Phases	All Phases
Integration of Deliverables	*Work-in-Progress Review*	All Phases	All Phases
Preparing for Approval or Funding Tollgates	*Work-in-Progress Review*	All Phases	All Phases
Post-Implementation Review	*Work-in-Progress Review*	Solution Delivery	Control

References

Best Practices, LLC (2000). *Benchmarking project management: Performance, measurement, processes and tools.* Chapel Hill, NC: Author.

DeMarco, T., & Lister, T. (1987). *Peopleware: Productive projects and teams.* New York: Dorset House.

Eckes, G. (2003). *Six sigma team dynamics: The elusive key to project success.* Hoboken, NJ: John Wiley & Sons.

Jones, C. (2000). *Software assessments, benchmarks, and best practices.* Reading, MA: Addison-Wesley.

Means, J., & Adams, T. (2005). *Facilitating the project lifecycle: Skills & tools to accelerate progress for project managers, facilitators and six sigma project teams.* San Francisco, CA: Jossey-Bass.

Tammy Adams *is currently the managing partner of Chaosity LLC and specializes in team facilitation and business process analysis. As a certified facilitator, Ms. Adams guides teams in identifying and transforming their process knowledge and business requirements into viable project and system deliverables that incorporate quality principles consistent with methodologies such as TQM, Six Sigma, and Lean. Ms. Adams' background includes extensive experience in project management, operations management, consulting services, training, and facilitation.*

Jan Means *is president of Resource Advantage, Inc., a consulting and training firm specializing in business process innovation, organization and information technology planning and design. Her special expertise is in facilitation of work sessions in large-scale project environments that bring business professionals together with information technology, project, and quality professionals to improve business performance.*

Giving Feedback to Leaders
Avoiding the Traps
Jan M. Schmuckler and Thomas J. Ucko

Summary

Giving clear and direct feedback to leaders is important to the success of the coaching experience. For HRD practitioners and external coaches who provide coaching services to organizations, this is a critical point. Yet there can be significant pitfalls along the way. This article examines some of the traps encountered during the feedback phase of coaching and offers HRD practitioners an opportunity to look at ways they could miss the mark. The article also highlights some of the strategies for preventing and remedying the identified traps and recommends that the HRD practitioner explore some new behaviors when delivering feedback.

The feedback phase is at the heart of the coaching process and one of the most critical phases in the coaching model. When the feedback phase is not executed skillfully, the entire assignment can go awry. This article highlights four key traps that coaches can fall into when giving feedback to clients and offers some strategies to avoid these traps.

Those who coach—whether HRD practitioners, organizational consultants, or full-time coaches—need to hold up a mirror to the client's behavior, even when the feedback is very difficult to share or hear. (*Note:* To simplify, from here forward we will refer to all those providing coaching, whatever their discipline, as "coaches.") Yet, for a variety of reasons, giving feedback presents problems for many coaches. This became real for us at a professional conference several years ago. In one workshop, the presenter gave the participants a case study to "work" in which a coach had collected information about the CEO. Later in the session, several participants, in turn, role played giving feedback to the "CEO" in front of the audience. Without exception, each of the role players softened the feedback or downplayed its importance. What was going on here? This wasn't even a real situation, and yet the coaches were holding back. We concluded that the process of giving feedback is problematic for many coaches, perhaps especially when the client is a high-level, "important" person—even if the individual is only role playing a CEO!

We believe that the feedback phase has high potential for coaches to critically re-think and revise some of their behaviors. In the next section of the article, we focus on four of the traps and also on the strategies to overcome these common pitfalls.

1. Failing to Prepare the Client

The Trap

Coaches sometimes assume that clients welcome feedback and that they want to work on improving their behaviors. Otherwise, why would they be in coaching? Yet clients are often less than enthusiastic about some of the data that the coach is presenting. The mis-taken assumption on the coaches' part occurs, especially when they are excited about the information and the consistency of the messages that they have collected. According to *What Did You Say? The Art of Giving and Receiving Feedback* (Seashore, Seashore, & Weinberg, 1991), the myth is that "if feedback has all the correct ingredients in its de-livery—clear, specific, timed right, non-judgmental, and speaks only to behavior—it will be accepted as given." However, we know that clients actually choose what they will ac-cept and what, if anything, they will do about the information and that preparing the client ahead of time will increase the chances of acceptance. By not adequately prepar-ing the client, coaches can fall into the trap of getting less acceptance of the feedback and more anger or more resistance.

The Strategy

It is the responsibility of coaches to make the feedback process known and visible to their clients. Coaches who prepare for feedback sessions with clients by helping their clients understand the feedback process are more successful. Preparation may include discussing the feedback process with the client prior to sharing the data and/or deter-mining which models will be useful for the client to fully appreciate the feedback in-formation. Pictures or models can be "worth a thousand words."

Sometimes we find it helpful to remind clients of the "1 percent rule." This "rule," invented by one of our colleagues, states that no matter how strongly the client dis-agrees with the feedback, no matter how much the feedback seems off-target, the client is to assume that at least 1 percent of the feedback is accurate.

Often the Johari Window is used to help clients understand that they have blind spots (Luft, 1982). With this model, coaches can prepare their clients for what kinds of feedback they will be receiving. Another way to prepare clients is by asking them what they typically do when they hear feedback and then having them describe a situation from their previous experience. For example, a VP of sales in a biotech company told the coach that in his previous company he usually would disregard feedback if he did not respect the source or if he thought the person had an axe to grind or was using the feedback for political gain. The coach assured the client that in this case there was no political gain or axe to grind so that the client could take in the feedback. Some additional questions coaches can ask clients include: "Are you willing to entertain a new way of listening?" "Are you willing to suspend your beliefs about how accurate the data is?" "Are you willing to stop yourself from guessing who said what?"

These tactics can be very useful when the coach senses that the client is resistant to receiving disconfirming information. Often the client is asked at the beginning of the data-collection phase—or even in the contracting phase—how he or she likes to receive feedback. It's a good idea to ask again when preparing for feedback.

In a large non-profit, Vickie, a client who did not like to hear "bad" feedback, told the coach in the preparation phase to give her positive feedback first, then give corrective feedback, and end with a more positive summary. This was useful information for organizing the feedback session. Additionally, Vickie was told the steps of the feedback stage, including what happens after the feedback is given. She learned that she would have a few days to digest the data and that her coach would give her support after she had time to reflect on the feedback. By knowing all the steps involved, she accepted the feedback very well, including what she saw as "bad" feedback. Some clients need a lot of preparation and others need less, depending on how they receive feedback and their level of trust.

2. Flooding the Client with Data

The Trap

Most 360-degree processes generate an enormous amount of data. As coaches, we may feel that all of the information can be useful to the client. The trap for coaches is that clients can become so overwhelmed by the large amount of data that they don't take it in, or else they discount it and don't take it seriously.

The Strategy

Coaches often have to decide what feedback is really useful for their clients and what information is redundant or not important to focus on at the time. When conducting interviews, coaches generally receive more information than the client can handle.

Coaches can choose the information that will be most useful for the client and stay focused in the feedback session on these key elements. For example, it is useful to pull out three key strengths and three to five key challenges that the client is facing.

When using a 360-degree instrument rather than interviews, the coach can engage the client in deciding what information is most relevant and useful. By asking questions such as "What stands out?" or "What surprises you?" the coach can begin a collaborative process of identifying the most important information. Either way, with interviews or surveys, focusing on a limited amount of data will ensure greater success with the coaching assignment.

In one coaching assignment, the coach provided the client with a bulleted list of six "areas for improvement." This was a case where the client educated the coach. The client asked, "How can I possibly focus on changing six things at once?" He was absolutely right, of course, and the coach learned a valuable lesson.

3. Failing to Deal with Resistance

The Trap

Often, even with the coach's best efforts at preparation, clients will resist accepting feedback. Like all of us, our clients have blind spots. They have self-perceptions that don't match how others see them. A significant part of our job as coaches is to shed light on these blind spots and help our clients see themselves as others see them. Yet when faced with challenges to a deeply held self-image, they may display anger, justify their behaviors as necessary, or claim that, whatever it is, they don't do it anymore. By falling into the trap of failing to deal with the client's resistance, coaches collude with the client and severely limit the possibilities of a successful coaching assignment.

The Strategy

The most effective strategy to deal with client resistance is to notice and call attention to the client's behavior. For example, in a recent coaching assignment, the coach collected 360-degree feedback on his CEO client that included a strong consensus that the CEO had great difficulty hearing bad news. As the client read the feedback summary, he slammed the pages down on the conference table and shouted, "I don't want to hear this!" The coach waited a moment and then said, "What you just did . . . that's what they're talking about." At first the CEO said nothing. After a long pause, he finally said, in a quiet voice, "Oh." The coach asked the CEO if this was how he typically reacted to bad news. Looking somewhat embarrassed, he replied, "Well, it's not usually this extreme." When asked what impact he thought even a less extreme negative reaction to bad news might have on his staff, the CEO grudgingly acknowledged that it could inhibit people from telling him about situations for which his action was needed. The coach's willingness to deal with the client's resistance allowed the coaching to proceed past what might otherwise have been a difficult impasse and resulted in significant learning for the client.

4. Avoiding or Softening Tough Feedback

The Trap

Giving feedback that significantly contradicts the client's self-perception can be difficult in the best of circumstances. We may hold back from giving straightforward and direct feedback. We may "pull our punches" and soften our feedback or avoid it entirely, fearing the client may become angry or dislike us. For internal coaches, this tendency may increase if the client's position is several steps above the coach's in the organization's hierarchy. External coaches may fear losing the assignment. In either case, coaches may allow clients with strong or aggressive personalities to intimidate them.

The Strategy

Certainly, preparing the client, as described in the strategy for the first trap above, is critical. It is equally important for coaches to prepare themselves. How can you do this? Here are some possibilities. First, anticipate the client's reactions. Based on previous interactions with the client, what is he or she likely to do or say when receiving difficult-to-hear feedback? Consider various possibilities. For each one, come up with a strategy for dealing with it. Then practice, either by mentally rehearsing your responses or by role playing with a trusted colleague.

Another way to prepare yourself is by addressing your own fears and concerns. Many of us have outdated "self-talk," silent inner dialogue or beliefs left over from childhood that suggest we will fold or feel bad when subjected to another's anger or rejection. For example, if we notice strong feelings of anxiety when planning to give a client "tough" feedback, this may indicate an underlying belief that we can't handle a powerful negative response from the client. In this case, it will be useful to "dispute" the belief by imagining the worst-case scenario and reminding ourselves that we can deal with such a situation and have successfully dealt with such situations in the past.

A Note on In-the-Moment Feedback

Feedback is not limited to the feedback phase. It is often useful to give "in-the-moment" feedback to a client as the behavior is happening. Giving feedback in real time creates a "coachable moment" and can give the client insights that might not otherwise occur. For example, at a coaching session with a chief technology officer (CTO) in his office, the coach noticed that, during the conversation, the CTO periodically looked down at papers on his desk. The coach called attention to what the CTO was doing and wondered aloud whether this behavior might account for the feedback from the CTO's reports that he didn't seem interested in their concerns. The CTO immediately recognized the connection and committed himself to focusing his attention on whomever he was with.

Summary

Feedback is essential to coaching. It gives clients insights into their own behavior that may have been unknown to them and helps clients understand how others see them. How coaches deliver feedback is critical to its acceptance and usefulness. In this article, we have examined some of the key traps encountered during the important "feedback" phase of coaching. In addition, we have presented strategies for preventing and remedying the identified traps. We hope this article will stimulate coaches to reexamine their behaviors during the feedback phase and try some new ones.

References

Luft, J. (1982). The Johari window: A graphic model of awareness in interpersonal relations. *Reading book for human relations training.* Alexandria, VA: NTL Institute for Applied Behavioral Science.

Seashore, C.N., Seashore, E.W., & Weinberg, G.M. (1991). *What did you say? The art of giving and receiving feedback.* North Attleborough, MA: Douglas Charles Press.

Jan M. Schmuckler, *organizational psychologist and leadership coach, works with executives and managers to achieve outstanding business results. Her more than twenty-five years of experience with leading companies in high technology, biotechnology, and financial sectors around the world brings unique perspectives for competing more effectively. Currently, Dr. Schmuckler is director of the Coaching Certificate Program at John F. Kennedy University, as well as heading her own consulting firm. Her Ph.D. in organizational psychology is from the Wright Institute.*

Thomas J. Ucko *is a leadership coach and organizational consultant who assists leaders and leadership teams to reach their potential and achieve their business goals. His clients range from global enterprises to startups. Mr. Ucko also teaches in the Coaching Certificate program at John F. Kennedy University and is the author of* Selecting and Working with Consultants: A Guide for Clients. *He holds an MBA from Fordham University and an MA in counseling psychology from Columbia University.*

How to Persuade Employees to Buy In to Change

Charles B. Royal

Summary

Getting buy-in from employees has always been the key to successful change, but the methods used have not worked very well. This author asks managers to see their employees as internal customers and to consider change as a new product, and he shows managers how to sell the change to employees by using time-tested, proven marketing principles and tools.

The most important factor in successful change management is employee buy-in. The reason is simple. It's employees who do the work to put the change in place.

If you don't have employee buy-in to change, nothing else you do really matters. No other actions will compensate for the lack of buy-in. On the other hand, if you do have employees who buy-in to change, nothing else is really necessary.

What Is Buy-In?

"Buy-in" is a word that is freely used in discussing change, yet buy-in is not in the dictionary. It has no official meaning. I define buy-in as *the willingness, and the ability, to do the work to make the change happen.*

How to Gain Employee Buy-In

Managers have used three traditional methods to gain employee buy-in:

- *Obligation.* Employees are on the payroll and have an obligation to support changes proposed by management.

- *Make a strong case for change.* Here, justification for the change is passed down from upper management, explaining why the organization needs the change.

- *Force.* Using force is essentially saying that employees must support the change or suffer the consequences.

These methods of obtaining buy-in have not worked very well. In an article on organizational change published in the *Harvard Business Review,* the authors concluded that, "Most (change) initiatives . . . have had low success rates. The brutal fact is that about 70 percent of all change initiatives fail" (Beer & Nohria, 2000). In my view, a 70 percent failure rate in something as important as change is unacceptable. It's time to try something new.

In today's environment, the only way to get employees to buy in to change is to *persuade* them.

Persuasion Tools

The most effective persuasion tools come from marketing and sales. I have identified the marketing and sales tools that are the most successful in persuading people to buy products and services. I then show managers how to use these tools to persuade employees, as internal customers, to buy in to change.

This is a natural extension of marketing because the same techniques can be used with internal customers as are used with external customers. The difference is that, instead of persuading external customers to buy your product, you're persuading your internal customers to buy in to the changes you want to make.

The reason this approach works is because marketing works. That's why all businesses do it. Marketing has developed to the point where the tools and techniques used to persuade people to buy things are time-tested and proven to produce results. This same marketing success can be used to persuade employees to buy in to the changes you want to make.

How People Make Buying Decisions

To persuade people to buy your product or service, you have to know why people buy and why people do not buy.

Before explaining these principles, and how to apply them to change, here are several behavioral rules that must be understood:

- The primary motivator of human behavior is the desire to be better off after the action than one was prior to the action. Marketers present their product/ service as an improvement over the customer's current situation.

- Customers must see the improved situation as being possible to achieve. There is no sense in trying to sell a Rolls Royce to someone who cannot afford one.

- People define products/services in their own terms, not the vendor's terms. They assign value according to what they think they are buying.

- People do not buy the features of a product—they buy the benefits. Benefits have value to the customer; features may or may not be used.

These behavioral rules are as applicable for persuading employees to buy in to a change as they are to persuading people to buy a product or service.

Why People Buy

People buy when they perceive the value of the product or service to them is greater than the price being asked for it. In other words, having the product is a better option than keeping their money. Marketing is an exchange process, and so is buying in to change. Products and services have a price, and so does change.

Getting buy-in requires a balance of interests between employees and managers. The first thing to look for is how the change can be structured or described in terms that will provide a benefit to employees that is close to the price they will have to pay. This may also require sacrifice by management to bring the balance in line.

As a manager, the key is to ask yourself, "Would I buy in to this change if I were an employee?" Remember, the first thought everyone has when change is proposed is "What's in it for me?"

People Buy Because the Seller Has Made It Easy for Them to Do So

Sellers do this in two ways. First, the seller removes barriers to the sale. For example, providing parking eliminates the inconvenience barrier; providing credit plans overcomes the inability to pay barrier.

In change situations, one of the common barriers is inconsistency that conflicts with the change. Employees recognize inconsistencies right away and use them as reasons not to support a change. The most common inconsistency is to propose a change, but retain policies that reward supporting the status quo.

Second, one of the most effective sales tools is to identify potential objections to the sale and address them in advance, as part of the sales process.

This is also an excellent tactic for persuading employees to buy in to change. Potential objections to change are usually pretty obvious. For example, the universal concern employees have about a proposed change is more work. Implementing change almost always involves more work because implementing change is usually added on top of existing work.

Assuming more work is a significant issue, there are two things that can be done to address the issue in advance. First, acknowledge it; admit to the staff that extra time and effort will be required. Second, do something about it. Depending on the situation, this could involve hiring additional help, allowing comp time on completion, or providing financial rewards. Any action taken preemptively to make the process easier is appreciated by employees and creates the goodwill you need for early buy-in.

Acknowledging and addressing objections in advance points out a unique characteristic of change management—the importance of doing it right the first time. If a change initiative starts out badly, you rarely recover from the hole that's been dug. Efforts to correct problems that should have been anticipated are not greeted with the same appreciation as if they were addressed up-front.

People Buy Because Others Influence Them

People will shortcut personal investigation of a product by relying on someone else they trust. This can be a friend, a testimonial, or an endorsement.

In change, influence is used in the form of opinion leaders. Identifying opinion leaders in an organization, and persuading them to buy in to the change first, can be the key to success. The goal is to have opinion leaders as fully informed spokespeople for the change. If employees hear solid answers from people they trust, buy-in is far more likely.

Why People Do Not Buy

In addition to the price/value disparity, *people do not buy because there is too much risk.* Risk comes in several forms, all of which apply to change:

- Being stuck with a bad purchase;

- Having to make an irreversible decision, for example, buying a non-returnable item;

- The size of the purchase or the amount at stake—the larger the purchase, the more risk is seen; and

- Lack of trust in the seller to perform as promised.

People make buying decisions that minimize their risk. They want to make a safe choice or avoid making a bad choice. Either way, they prefer the known over the unknown. Traveling through a new city at lunchtime, there is less risk in eating at McDonald's than there is in stopping at a local restaurant.

The marketing principle is this: Reduce the risk from the purchase, and the chances a person will buy increase proportionately.

There are direct applications of this principle in securing employee buy-in. Change always involves risk, and employees will see that risk. The first step is to look at things from the employees' perspective and identify the risks they see. Acknowledge these risks and reduce them on a preemptive basis whenever possible:

- If the bad purchase or irreversible decision risks apply, promise to evaluate the change at a specific time in the future. Point out that employees do not have to buy in to the entire change, just the first steps. If appropriate, include the staff in the evaluation. When you do this, the chances of being stuck with a bad change are reduced.

- If the size of the change is an issue, plan to take smaller, incremental steps instead of one big one. Evaluate progress regularly along the way. When there is real doubt, take the smallest first step possible. Mid-course corrections are another valuable tool in reducing risk.

- Lack of trust in the "seller" can be addressed by selecting a respected person to lead the change effort. This person must have a solid reputation and track record. A person employees feel will force change on them or who will be crafting the change for personal benefit will not be trusted. Who you buy from is important. Who you buy in from is equally important.

Dealing with Competition

All businesses have competitors. It is management's responsibility to know who their competition is and to be sure their business offers a better choice for current and prospective customers.

In change, the main competition is the *status quo*. If you want to persuade employees to buy in to change, you have to offer a better alternative than the current situation.

The way to do this is to do a competitive analysis and apply it to the situation you're trying to change. The information gained from a competitive analysis will go further to assure successful change than almost any other step you can take. The price for this success is that the questions are penetrating and that the answers require objectivity.

The following are questions commonly asked when doing a competitive analysis in marketing. As you will see, they are equally effective for analyzing how internal customers see their current situation and for how a proposed change compares to it.

Elements of a Competitive Analysis

- Who/what is the competition? In change, the competition is the status quo, but the status quo of what?

- Is it a specific procedure or something as broad as corporate culture?

- What do current customers like about the competitor's product? In change, what do employees like about the current situation? This answer will indicate the strength of the status quo. Try to retain as many things employees like as possible. Point out to employees what is not changing so that they see the change in the proper context.

- What do current customers dislike about the competitor's product? What problems are they having with it? In change, find problems the change would solve and/or what benefits and improvements would result.

- What are the competitor's strengths and weaknesses? In the external market, this could be costs, technology, service, or other non-price factors. In change, these can be historical issues, cultural norms, past performance, or successes and failures.

- What options do current customers have? In change, the first option employees have is staying or leaving. This can depend on the current job climate, that is, are other jobs available? Who has the option of leaving, and who does not? What impact will this have on the change process?

- What are the rules of the game, written and unwritten? In change, consider cultural factors and corporate policies and procedures that would get in the way of the change. Pay special attention to inconsistencies that would provide employees a reason not to support the change.

- How well is the competition doing? If things are going well, that is, with market share or financial results, the pull of the status quo will be very strong ("if it's not broken, don't fix it"). If results are deteriorating, there is more reason to change.

- What are the economics? Is the competition financially strong? In change, there are always employee security issues. It may help to point out how this could change in the future if action is not taken now.

- How do customers make the buying decision in choosing between vendors? In change, it comes down to determining how employees would make the decision to buy in. What factors would most influence their decision?

- Knowing what we know, what kind of a defense or new product will the competition throw up against us? The competition is not going to just sit there and let us take away their business. When you are making a change, realistically determine what the issues will be from the employees' perspective. Can any of these be addressed in advance?

New Product Development and Marketing

Just as we can view employees as internal customers for change, we can consider change as a new product—something employees have not used before and probably don't know much about.

New product development and marketing has been the subject of widespread research for the last thirty years. The goal has been to find the keys to persuading people to buy new products. The results are directly applicable to change and provide many more tools to use in persuading employees to buy in to change.

Key Product Findings

The most significant finding was that new product success is not the result of luck. It is predictable and controllable. When certain keys are applied, new products can expect a 75 percent success rate! Using the same keys in change initiatives can significantly increase the change success rate.

Another finding was that *product development and the marketing of those products are intertwined, rather than separate functions.* The lesson is that, when planning a change, a vital part of the process is to decide how you're going to sell the change to employees.

Last, while the execution of each step in the new product process is crucial, *the first few plays of the game determine the outcome.* When undergoing change processes also, it is important to start out right. Methods for selling new products give us many tools to do that.

Lessons for Success

Robert G. Cooper (1993), in his book, *Winning at New Products,* points out the lessons learned from new product research. Several of them can be used in planning change.

The number-one success factor for selling new products is having *a product that delivers unique benefits and superior value to the customer.* Superior value must be defined from the customer's standpoint, not the design department's.

The real emphasis is on benefits. Customers pay for benefits that relate to their needs, wants, problems, likes, and dislikes. And the benefits must be more attractive than those of other competitive offerings.

This finding ties back to the discussion of why people buy and why they do not buy. It also points out the value of doing a competitive analysis and a risk assessment.

The lesson for managing change is that, if a proposed change does not solve a problem for those affected or improve their situation, it's time to rethink the change. The chances of getting buy-in, and of successfully implementing the change, are very small.

The number two success factor is having *a sharp product definition early in the development process.* Sharply defined products had over three times the success rate of less defined products.

In marketing, product definition includes who the intended users are, the benefits to be delivered, and a list of the product's features, requirements, and specifications. Solid product definition speeds up the change process too because everyone is on the same page. With a poorly defined change product, people waste time clarifying what to do and often have to cycle back. The process can even come to a standstill because, when employees are in doubt, the tendency is to do nothing.

The starting point is to define/describe the change in marketing terms. If you want employees to buy in to a change, consider what you're asking them to buy. Instead of a pure definition of the change, describe it in terms of what it will accomplish or what it will be like when the change in finally implemented.

Another reason for describing change in marketing terms is word of mouth. The one certainty about change is that employees will talk about it. How you describe the change initially determines what they will say. Will they be talking negatively about the difficulties, or will they be talking positively about the outcome?

A third lesson is that *more predevelopment work must be done before product development begins.* The steps that precede the actual design and development of the product are key factors separating winners from losers and lead to better product definition.

When change is treated in the same way, it's important to take the time to review why people buy and why they don't buy, to identify the potential objections in advance, to identify and reduce risks wherever possible, and to define the change in marketing terms. Despite the inclination to push the change process ahead, doing the predevelopment work actually results in earlier buy-in and faster implementation.

This leads to the last product development lesson—*speed is everything, but not at the expense of quality execution.* In our fast-paced world, speed can be a competitive weapon. However, research has shown that companies that bring a product to market quickly by short-cutting the predevelopment steps incur product reliability and service/warranty problems that can destroy profits. The lesson is to do it right the first time.

This is one of our main messages in this article. Doing it right the first time is not only the key to gaining buy-in for the current change, but doing it right each time is the key to repeat business. When change is managed well, employees will be more willing to buy in to future changes because a positive precedent has been set. They begin to trust the process.

Conclusion

Change is the primary force affecting organizations today. The key to successful change is getting employees to buy in to changes that must be made. The sooner employees buy in, the sooner the change will be implemented. The only way to do this is to persuade them.

Marketing and sales are a good source of information on effective persuasion. At the start of every change initiative, managers must ask, "How are we going to 'sell' this change to the employees?" By identifying the marketing principles and tools that apply to that particular change and building them into the roll-out plans, the chances that employees will buy in to the change increase dramatically.

References

Beer, M., & Nohria, N. (2000, May/June). Cracking the code of change. *Harvard Business Review.*

Cooper, R.G. (1993). *Winning at new products.* Reading, MA: Perseus Books.

Charles B. Royal *is the founder of Change Directions. After thirty-five years as an insurance executive, he began a second career in change management. He recognized the importance of buy-in to successful change and created the "Buying In to Change" program that shows managers how to persuade employees to buy in to the changes they want to make by using marketing tools and techniques. The material in this article is taken from that program.*

Contributors

Tammy Adams
Chaosity LLC
8611 South Kachina Drive
Tempe, AZ 85284
    (480) 775-8756
    fax: (480) 422-9095
    email: tadams@chaosity.com

Kristin J. Arnold, CMC, CPF, CSP
Quality Process Consultants, Inc.
11304 Megan Drive
Fairfax, VA 22030
    (703) 278-0892
    fax: (703) 278-0891
    email: karnold@qpcteam.com

Beverly J. Bitterman
5307 Winhawk Way
Lutz, FL 33558
    (813) 964-1260
    fax: (813) 961-7062
    email: beverly@beverlybitterman.com

Cheryl A. Brown
Inspirational Learning Solutions Group
3936 S. Semoran Boulevard, #482
Orlando, FL 32822
    (321) 438-8004
    email: gwbf.cbrown@att.net

Chris W. Chen
1209 Gold Flower Road
Carlsbad, CA 92009
    (858) 654-1841
    email: cchen@semprautilities.com

Peter R. Garber
PPG Industries, Inc.
One PPG Place
Pittsburgh, PA 15272
    (412) 434-2009
    fax: (412) 434-3490
    email: garber@ppg.com

Barbara Pate Glacel, Ph.D.
12103 Richland Lane
Oak Hill, VA 20171
    (703) 262-9120
    email: BPGlacel@glacel.com
    URL: www.glacel.com

Dr. K.S. Gupta
HAL Management Academy
Viamanpura Post
Bangalore, Karnataka (PIN) 560017
India
    +91-80-25233133
    fax: +91-80-25236598
    email: ksgupta37@hotmail.com

Nichola D. Gutgold
Assistant Professor of Communication,
  Arts and Sciences
Penn State Berks-Lehigh Valley College
8380 Mohr Lane
Fogelsville, PA 18051
  (610) 285-5101
  email: dgn2@psu.edu

Gail Hahn, MA, CSP, CPRP, CLL
Fun*cilitators
11407 Orchard Green Court
Reston, VA 20190
  (866) fun.at.work (866-386-2896)
  or (703) 707-0468
  fax: (530) 326-2979
  email: gail@funcilitators.com
  URL: www.funcilitators.com

Jane Hascall
Hascall Consulting
12538 West First Place
Lakewood, CO 80228
  (303) 980-9254
  email: janehascall@sprintmail.com

Cher Holton, Ph.D.
The Holton Consulting Group, Inc.
4704 Little Falls Drive, Suite 300
Raleigh, NC 27609
  (919) 783-7088
  (800) 336-3940
  fax: (919) 781-2218
  email: cher@holtonconsulting.com

H.B. Karp
Associate Professor
Hampton University, Department
  of Management
Hampton, VA 23668
  (757) 488-3536
  email: pgshank@aol.com

Teri B. Lund
Strategic Assessment and Evaluation
  Associates, LLC
5015 SW Lodi
Portland, OR 97221
  (503) 245-9020
  email: tlund_bls@msn.com

Rick Maurer
Maurer & Associates
5653 8th Street North
Arlington, VA 22205
  (703) 525-7074
  email: rick@beyondresistance.com
  URL: www.beyondresistance.com

Jan Means
Resource Advantage, Inc.
284 Ford Road
Melrose, NY 12121
  (518) 663-5232
  fax: (518) 663-5233
  email: janmeans@aol.com

Mohandas K. Nair
A2 Kamdar Building
607, Gokhale Road (South), Dadar
Mumbai, Maharashtra 400028
India
  91-022-24226307
  email: mknair@vsnl.net

Bridget A. O'Brien
1818 Pennland Court
Lansdale, PA 19446
  (215) 368-4447
  email: bridget_obrien@merck.com

Edwina Pio, Ph.D.
Auckland University of Technology
Faculty of Business
Mer-Level 2, 46 Wakefield Street
Private Bag 92006
Auckland 1020
New Zealand
  +64-9-9179999, ext. 5130
  fax: +64-9-9179884
  email: epio@aut.ac.nz

Greg Robinson, Ph.D.
Challenge Quest, LLC
P.O. Box 396
Pryor, OK 74362
  (918) 825-4711
  email: greg@challengequest.com

Mark Rose
11729 Cedar Valley Drive
Oklahoma City, OK 73170
  (405) 323-1522
  email: rosemg@oge.com

Charles B. Royal
Change Directions
2840 Marledge Street
Madison, WI 53711
  (608) 273-9559
  email: royal8@charter.net

Jan M. Schmuckler, Ph.D.
3921 Burckhalter Avenue
Oakland, CA 94605
  (510) 562-0626
  email: jan@lignumvitae.com
  URL: www.janconsults.com

Beverly Scott
Bev Scott Consulting
166 Castro Street
San Francisco, CA 94114
  (415) 863-2994
  email: bev@bevscott.com

Elizabeth A. Smith, Ph.D.
Executive Director
CRG Medical Foundation
  for Patient Safety
6800 West Loop South, Suite 190
Bellaire, TX 77401
  (281) 497-8876
  fax: (281) 920-1118
  email: esmith@crgmedical.com

Marilyn J. Sprague-Smith, M.Ed.
Miracles & Magic, Inc.
308 Misty Waters Lane
Jamestown, NC 27282-8859
  (336) 454-8750
  fax: (336) 454-8923
  email:
  marilyn@miraclesmagicinc.com

Thomas J. Ucko
602 Chapman Drive
Corte Madera, CA 94925
  (415) 924-7010
  email: tom@ucko.com
  URL: www.ucko.com

Mary B. Wacker, M.S.
M.B. Wacker Associates
3175 N. 79th Street
Milwaukee, WI 53222-3930
   (414) 875-9876
   fax: (414) 875-9874
   email: mary@mbwacker.com

Kathryn Carson Key Whitehead
1857 Laurel Ridge Drive
Nashville, TN 37215
   (615) 665-1138
   fax: (615) 665-8902
   email: digmypig@aol.com

Devora D. Zack
President, Only Connect Consulting, Inc.
7806 Ivymount Terrace
Potomac, MD 20854
   (301) 765-6262
   fax: (301) 765-2182
   email: dzack@onlyconnect.biz

Contents of the Companion Volume, *The 2006 Pfeiffer Annual: Training*

Editor's Choice

Inventories, Questionnaires, and Surveys

Articles and Discussion Resources

**Topic is cutting edge.

How to Use the CD-ROM

System Requirements

PC with Microsoft Windows 98SE or later
Mac with Apple OS version 8.6 or later

Using the CD with Windows

To view the items located on the CD, follow these steps:

1. Insert the CD into your computer's CD-ROM drive.

2. A window appears with the following options:

    Contents: Allows you to view the files included on the CD-ROM.

    Software: Allows you to install useful software from the CD-ROM.

    Links: Displays a hyperlinked page of websites.

    Author: Displays a page with information about the Author(s).

    Contact Us: Displays a page with information on contacting the publisher or author.

    Help: Displays a page with information on using the CD.

    Exit: Closes the interface window.

If you do not have autorun enabled, or if the autorun window does not appear, follow these steps to access the CD:

1. Click Start -> Run.

2. In the dialog box that appears, type d:<\\>start.exe, where d is the letter of your CD-ROM drive. This brings up the autorun window described in the preceding set of steps.

3. Choose the desired option from the menu. (See Step 2 in the preceding list for a description of these options.)

In Case of Trouble

If you experience difficulty using the CD-ROM, please follow these steps:

1. Make sure your hardware and systems configurations conform to the systems requirements noted under "System Requirements" above.

2. Review the installation procedure for your type of hardware and operating system.

It is possible to reinstall the software if necessary.

To speak with someone in Product Technical Support, call 800-762-2974 or 317-572-3994 M–F 8:30 a.m.–5:00 p.m. EST. You can also get support and contact Product Technical Support through our website at www.wiley.com/techsupport.

Before calling or writing, please have the following information available:

- Type of computer and operating system

- Any error messages displayed

- Complete description of the problem.

It is best if you are sitting at your computer when making the call.

Pfeiffer Publications Guide

This guide is designed to familiarize you with the various types of Pfeiffer publications. The formats section describes the various types of products that we publish; the methodologies section describes the many different ways that content might be provided within a product. We also provide a list of the topic areas in which we publish.

FORMATS

In addition to its extensive book-publishing program, Pfeiffer offers content in an array of formats, from fieldbooks for the practitioner to complete, ready-to-use training packages that support group learning.

FIELDBOOK Designed to provide information and guidance to practitioners in the midst of action. Most fieldbooks are companions to another, sometimes earlier, work, from which its ideas are derived; the fieldbook makes practical what was theoretical in the original text. Fieldbooks can certainly be read from cover to cover. More likely, though, you'll find yourself bouncing around following a particular theme, or dipping in as the mood, and the situation, dictate.

HANDBOOK A contributed volume of work on a single topic, comprising an eclectic mix of ideas, case studies, and best practices sourced by practitioners and experts in the field.

An editor or team of editors usually is appointed to seek out contributors and to evaluate content for relevance to the topic. Think of a handbook not as a ready-to-eat meal, but as a cookbook of ingredients that enables you to create the most fitting experience for the occasion.

RESOURCE Materials designed to support group learning. They come in many forms: a complete, ready-to-use exercise (such as a game); a comprehensive resource on one topic (such as conflict management) containing a variety of methods and approaches; or a collection of like-minded activities (such as icebreakers) on multiple subjects and situations.

TRAINING PACKAGE An entire, ready-to-use learning program that focuses on a particular topic or skill. All packages comprise a guide for the facilitator/trainer and a workbook for the participants. Some packages are supported with additional media—such as video—or learning aids, instruments, or other devices to help participants understand concepts or practice and develop skills.

- *Facilitator/trainer's guide* Contains an introduction to the program, advice on how to organize and facilitate the learning event, and step-by-step instructor notes. The guide also contains copies of presentation materials—handouts, presentations, and overhead designs, for example—used in the program.

- *Participant's workbook* Contains exercises and reading materials that support the learning goal and serves as a valuable reference and support guide for participants in the weeks and months that follow the learning event. Typically, each participant will require his or her own workbook.

ELECTRONIC CD-ROMs and web-based products transform static Pfeiffer content into dynamic, interactive experiences. Designed to take advantage of the searchability, automation, and ease-of-use that technology provides, our e-products bring convenience and immediate accessibility to your workspace.

METHODOLOGIES

CASE STUDY A presentation, in narrative form, of an actual event that has occurred inside an organization. Case studies are not prescriptive, nor are they used to prove a point; they are designed to develop critical analysis and decision-making skills. A case study has a specific time frame, specifies a sequence of events, is narrative in structure, and contains a plot structure—an issue (what should be/have been done?). Use case studies when the goal is to enable participants to apply previously learned theories to the circumstances in the case, decide what is pertinent, identify the real issues, decide what should have been done, and develop a plan of action.

ENERGIZER A short activity that develops readiness for the next session or learning event. Energizers are most commonly used after a break or lunch to stimulate or refocus the group. Many involve some form of physical activity, so they are a useful way to counter post-lunch lethargy. Other uses include transitioning from one topic to another, where "mental" distancing is important.

EXPERIENTIAL LEARNING ACTIVITY (ELA) A facilitator-led intervention that moves participants through the learning cycle from experience to application (also known as a Structured Experience). ELAs are carefully thought-out designs in which there is a definite learning purpose and intended outcome. Each step—everything that participants do during the activity—facilitates the accomplishment of the stated goal. Each ELA includes complete instructions for facilitating the intervention and a clear statement of goals, suggested group size and timing, materials required, an explanation of the process, and, where appropriate, possible variations to the activity. (For more detail on Experiential Learning Activities, see the Introduction to the *Reference Guide to Handbooks and Annuals*, 1999 edition, Pfeiffer, San Francisco.)

GAME A group activity that has the purpose of fostering team spirit and togetherness in addition to the achievement of a pre-stated goal. Usually contrived—undertaking a desert expedition, for example—this type of learning method offers an engaging means for participants to demonstrate and practice business and interpersonal skills. Games are effective for team building and personal development mainly because the goal is subordinate to the process—the means through which participants reach decisions, collaborate, communicate, and generate trust and understanding. Games often engage teams in "friendly" competition.

ICEBREAKER A (usually) short activity designed to help participants overcome initial anxiety in a training session and/or to acquaint the participants with one another. An icebreaker can be a fun activity or can be tied to specific topics or training goals. While a useful tool in itself, the icebreaker comes into its own in situations where tension or resistance exists within a group.

INSTRUMENT A device used to assess, appraise, evaluate, describe, classify, and summarize various aspects of human behavior. The term used to describe an instrument depends primarily on its format and purpose. These terms include survey, questionnaire, inventory, diagnostic survey, and poll. Some uses of instruments include providing instrumental feedback to group members, studying here-and-now processes or functioning within a group, manipulating group composition, and evaluating outcomes of training and other interventions.

Instruments are popular in the training and HR field because, in general, more growth can occur if an individual is provided with a method for focusing specifically on his or her own behavior. Instruments also are used to obtain information that will serve as a basis for change and to assist in workforce planning efforts.

Paper-and-pencil tests still dominate the instrument landscape with a typical package comprising a facilitator's guide, which offers advice on administering the instrument and interpreting the collected data, and an initial set of instruments. Additional instruments are available separately. Pfeiffer, though, is investing heavily in e-instruments. Electronic instrumentation provides effortless distribution and, for larger groups particularly, offers advantages over paper-and-pencil tests in the time it takes to analyze data and provide feedback.

LECTURETTE A short talk that provides an explanation of a principle, model, or process that is pertinent to the participants' current learning needs. A lecturette is intended to establish a common language bond between the trainer and the participants by providing a mutual frame of reference. Use a lecturette as an introduction to a group activity or event, as an interjection during an event, or as a handout.

MODEL A graphic depiction of a system or process and the relationship among its elements. Models provide a frame of reference and something more tangible, and more easily remembered, than a verbal explanation. They also give participants something to "go on," enabling them to track their own progress as they experience the dynamics, processes, and relationships being depicted in the model.

ROLE PLAY A technique in which people assume a role in a situation/scenario: a customer service rep in an angry-customer exchange, for example. The way in which the role is approached is then discussed and feedback is offered. The role play is often repeated using a different approach and/or incorporating changes made based on feedback received. In other words, role playing is a spontaneous interaction involving realistic behavior under artificial (and safe) conditions.

SIMULATION A methodology for understanding the interrelationships among components of a system or process. Simulations differ from games in that they test or use a model that depicts or mirrors some aspect of reality in form, if not necessarily in content. Learning occurs by studying the effects of change on one or more factors of the model. Simulations are commonly used to test hypotheses about what happens in a system—often referred to as "what if?" analysis—or to examine best-case/worst-case scenarios.

THEORY A presentation of an idea from a conjectural perspective. Theories are useful because they encourage us to examine behavior and phenomena through a different lens.

TOPICS

The twin goals of providing effective and practical solutions for workforce training and organization development and meeting the educational needs of training and human resource professionals shape Pfeiffer's publishing program. Core topics include the following:

Leadership & Management

Communication & Presentation

Coaching & Mentoring

Training & Development

e-Learning

Teams & Collaboration

OD & Strategic Planning

Human Resources

Consulting

What will you find on pfeiffer.com?

• The best in workplace performance solutions for training and HR professionals

• Downloadable training tools, exercises, and content

• Web-exclusive offers

• Training tips, articles, and news

• Seamless on-line ordering

• Author guidelines, information on becoming a Pfeiffer Affiliate, and much more

Discover more at www.pfeiffer.com